TOYS FOR GROWING:
A Guide to Toys
That Develop Skills

TOYS FOR GROWING:
A Guide to Toys That Develop Skills

MARY SINKER

Illustrated by Katherine Thomas

Published for

National Lekotek Center
Evanston, Illinois

YEAR BOOK MEDICAL PUBLISHERS, INC.
Chicago • London

0 9 8 7 6 5 4 3 2 1

ISBN 0–8151–7750-X

Copy Editor: Deborah Thorp
Design: Duncan R. Dickinson
Text Photography: Peggy Zarnek
Cover photo: f • 22, Inc.
Compositor: The Clarinda Company
Printing and Binding: Malloy Lithographing

Thanks to the Quaker Oats foundation for their generosity
in helping Lekotek produce the first edition of this book.

To J and D, my first toy teachers.

CONTENTS

INTRODUCTION

The toys in this guide have been carefully selected from the vast inventory at the National Lekotek Center. They represent the most stimulating, appealing, playful, and durable of the thousands considered.

Mary Sinker is the Program Director of the National Lekotek Center. The members of the Lekotek staff are recognized professionals, specializing in child development and early childhood education. Having purchased, analyzed, catalogued, and used thousands of toys for many years, they are also masters of intelligent toy selection.

note: Lekotek is always looking for new play materials to evaluate for subsequent editions of this toy guide. If you find an outstanding toy that you feel should be considered for inclusion, please let us know. Just drop us a note or postcard with the name of the toy, the manufacturer, the distributor, and a line or two stating why you like it. We'll try it out.

For information on the activities of the National Lekotek Center and the world-wide system of Lekoteks write to:

> National Lekotek Center
> Evanston Civic Center
> 2100 Ridge Avenue
> Evanston, IL 60204

Lekotek is an invented Swedish word for play-library and refers to a world wide system of resource centers for children with special needs and their families. All children, whether handicapped or non-handicapped, follow similar developmental sequences; and for all children, toys are the most powerful tools for learning. Children learn through play, and hidden in that play are the keys to stimulating a child's maximum development. Good toys function like masterful, ever present teachers.

HOW TO USE THIS BOOK

This book has been designed to be used equally well by parents looking for good toys for their child, grandparents buying a present, therapists searching for just the right toys for their clients, pre-school teachers and care providers finding toys to enrich their children's environments. While all the toys in the guide have been field tested with children with special needs, they are all toys that any children enjoy using.

The toys in this guide are organized by developmental category. Within each category the toys progress from the least difficult to the most difficult. The steps between levels of difficulty are tiny so that there is possibility for challenge at the same time that there is room for success.

Price ranges are given as a guide only, because prices change, often very quickly. The price code is:

A	$ 1—10
B	$11—20
C	$21—30
D	$31—40
E	$41—50
F	$51—75
G	$75—100
H	over $100

Because this book is designed to be used by individuals buying toys for one child and by professionals buying toys for an institution, a few words of explanation on how to buy these toys are necessary.

Following the description of each toy is a code that tells where the toy can be purchased.

Toys with Code 1 are widely available, often in stores that offer discounts.

Toys with Code 2 are available from specialty toy stores. Often, even if these toys aren't available in a small toy store near you, that store will be willing to order the toy for you from a wholesale supplier.

Toys with Code 3 are usually only available through catalog orders. The catalogs are all listed in the Resources Appendix at the back of the book.

Although all the toys in this guide have proven to be durable and safe while using, Lekotek does not accept liability for any damage or loss that may arise from their use. Lekotek has sole responsibility for the content of this book.

TOYS AND DEVELOPMENT

TOYS AND DEVELOPMENT

How do we know whether a particular toy is right for a specific child? To be able to match a toy to a child with a fair degree of accuracy, it is necessary to have an understanding of how children develop—physically, socially, and emotionally—and how these developing abilities match up to specific toys. This working knowledge of child development becomes even more important when choosing toys for a child with a handicap. The child's age isn't as important as the child's interests and abilities. In this brief text, normal age ranges have been used to define the boundaries of each stage, but for all children these ranges are extremely variable. While the ages will vary a great deal, the sequence of abilities will not.

0–2 Months: Settling and Seeing

In the early weeks after birth, the baby's primary focus is on learning about all the sensations of being alive. The human face closely talking, smiling, laughing, pausing, and going on again is the best possible plaything for the new baby. His play abilities are limited to being able to see and being able to hear. The baby's hearing is very keen, even as a newborn. In addition to the many music boxes available commercially, parents and caregivers should be aware that singing, whistling, and recordings of all kinds are enjoyable to the very young baby.

The very young baby can see accurately at the distance of 6"–8". Bright colors are most visible, as well as geometric shapes and designs. The contrast of yellow against dark blue, yellow against purple and yellow against black makes these the most visible colors. Because the baby's hands are usually tightly fisted he has no hand control. Expendable items can be hung for the baby to look at. Feathers, ribbons, cellophane and tinfoil are all bright and, for this age, safe. The book *Smart Toys* by Burtt and Kalkstein is a rich resource for learning how to make interesting toys for this and later stages.

The very young baby is still tied to the ''fencer's position'' by asymmetrical tonic neck reflex and can't hold his head in midline, so things for the baby to look at should be placed quite low and off to the side. Interesting toys for this age group are **Toys to Look At.**

2–4 Months: Random Movement, Discovery of Hands

At some time during the second month, parents of a new baby realize that this little bundle is beginning to be settled. The baby and the parent have started figuring each other out. The baby learns that his cries will be attended to; the parent learns what those cries mean—tired, hungry, lonely. More time is spent awake by *both* parties. The baby may even give up his middle-of-the-night feeding so that the mother isn't always looking for a chance to catch up on missed sleep.

Along with this mutual understanding come some rather dramatic physical changes. The baby unfolds. Where the new baby is a tightly compact lump with arms and legs flexed, the 2–4 month old's limbs extend and start to wave around. Prone, the baby of this age lifts his head up and looks around. He may begin to flip from stomach to back, and by the end of this period can hold his head in midline quite well.

While his hands are still often fisted, more and more they are open. Control of those open hands is minimal, but a keen observer will see the baby learning about his hands. At first it will not include visual activity. The baby will catch one hand with the other, clasp and unclasp them, twiddle the fingers. This will evolve into visual play with the hands. The baby will spend many happy minutes watching his hands wave about, bringing them together, measuring the distance from hand to hand, and finally, popping a finger or whole hand into his mouth. This is the beginning of hand/eye coordination, and once the mouth has been found with the hands, the baby enters a period of hand/eye/mouth coordination. *Everything* will eventually go to the mouth.

All of these physical changes, coupled with the fact that the baby is awake more of the time, give the parent/caregiver cues about play. Although the movement of the limbs is random, it *can* be capitalized on. For floor play, easy response toys can be used. **Toys to Bat At** are ideal for this stage. **Pull Toys** gently pulled across the baby's field of vision by an adult are interesting to the prone baby.

In an infant chair, hanging toys that respond to batting with sound and movement will be enjoyed. Because the head is more often in midline, mobiles hung over the crib will be enjoyed. The book *Smart Toys* can be recommended for several unique made-at-home playthings. The baby of this age is also verbally playful. He coos and babbles and will love a game of coo and babble with the parent, each talking his own language and waiting for the other to take a turn.

4–6 Months:
Refining Movement; Controlled Grasp

During these few months the changes the baby makes are not particularly dramatic. He doesn't learn to crawl, or to sit, or to walk, or to talk. Rather, this is a period when all of the baby's skills—social, verbal, and physical—are refined and strengthened, paving the way for dramatic change in the next few months.

In a supine position, the limbs that used to flail about now move rhythmically. Prone, the baby can get head and chest off the floor with ease and will even lift one hand and arm to reach toward a toy. In his infant chair, the baby will still play with his hands, but now, instead of greeting that waving hand with surprise, he purposefully watches his hand come in and out of his line of vision, and may even turn his head or head and body to look at the hand. Having become an excellent batter in earlier months, the baby uses those open hands to grasp, often making several attempts before being able to take an object.

Socially, this is the golden age of babyhood. Freed from most reflexive posture and behavior, and not yet into teething discomfort or stranger anxiety, the baby of this age is a social being. Smiles come easily and light up the whole body with sound and wriggles. Verbally, the baby is rarely silent. Consonants B, P, and M are sometimes added to the "ooo and aaa" sounds made earlier. Just as this is the golden age for babies, it's a time when parents/caregivers need to redefine their role. The first months are spent in a state of exhaustion from lack of sleep and the enormous physical requirements—primarily feeding and doing laundry—of the new baby. Later months will be spent making sure the increasingly mobile baby is safe wherever he travels. During *this* period the parent needs to learn how vital she is for the baby's entertainment. The 4–6 month old baby gets bored, and can't move to find new things to amuse himself. While he may be content on the floor for a few minutes, he eventually will wiggle or roll himself into a position he can't get out of. Put into a padded highchair with a tray full of toys, his immature grasp will quickly push the best toys on the floor. The parent will learn that she is needed to help the baby play, to move him from place to place, to present him with a changing array of toys and to facilitate his interaction with these toys. Rattles are great toys for this age. Because the baby isn't yet expert at waving the rattle to make sound, the rattle should be one that makes noise easily. The adult presenting the rattle should be patient and give the baby time to coordinate all his new skills and finally manage to reach and grasp.

Often the baby will begin his reach with his mouth wide open, almost gasping for the pleasure of the rattle. Although he may miss a few times, he will begin to bring everything to his mouth for additional exploration.

In addition to good easy sound, the rattle should be an appropriate size for the small baby's hands. Many of the rattles currently available are simply too big. Think carefully about size when choosing rattles. Easily squeezed latex toys are good because of their high tactile interest.

Because the baby's grasp is becoming increasingly accurate, all expendables—magazine pictures, ribbons, feathers, etc.—should be discarded for safety's sake. **Toys to Grasp and Handle,** as well as some **Suction Toys** are good for this stage.

6–8 Months: Begin Movement; Mouth Exploration

The baby of this age has two main preoccupations—his mouth and gaining some mobility.

Beginning at about 6 months and continuing for the next several months, everything the baby can grasp will go straight to his mouth before he does anything else with the object. The most musical of rattles will be explored with the mouth before being shaken and listened to, shaken and watched. The fact that teeth begin coming through during this period gives parents a handy excuse for all this mouthing: "He's teething." But even children whose teeth don't erupt until much later in their first year spend these months exploring with the part of their bodies they can control best—their mouths.

The range for achieving normal movement in children is quite large. Some babies will be making a slow, unsteady roll-stretch-roll progression of 3 feet at the same age other babies actually get up on their knees and take off. But there is a passion for moving at this age. Because they can flip from stomach to back, they will. They will then start practicing how to go from back to stomach. The baby will reach and push a little with his legs to get to an interesting object, eventually putting those motions all together into a crude body-arm-kick creep. He'll get his knees under him in one of the kicks and experiment with rocking on hands and knees. This will eventually all come together in a well-coordinated, high-speed crawl, but the key during these months is the baby's drive to achieve movement.

Playthings for this period are easy. For the mouth, provide texture.

There are many rattles with interesting texture on the market. **Toys to Grasp and Handle** are still favorites.

Playthings for the floor also abound. Because the baby can't make consistent progress on the floor, balls aren't good because they move away too easily. But stationary toys such as several of the early **Busy Boxes,** set just out of reach, are good for the baby to reach for and scooch toward. An interesting expendable toy for this age is a long strip of computer paper. (Because the baby can tear pieces and fill his mouth with them, this should only be used with the mom or dad around.) The baby will delight in crinkling the paper, rolling on the paper and playing little peek-a-boo games with the paper.

Socially, the 6–8 month old has made an astounding change. No longer does this friendly baby greet a stranger with smiles, squeals and wriggles. Rather, the new person is subjected to a rather solemn regard from the safe distance of Mom's shoulder. This baby knows who Mom is and, for the most part, only wants the people he knows. (The next step after the solemn regard of strangers is, of course, the crying and burying his face in the comfortable shoulder of the parent, but this usually comes a little later.)

This 6–8 month old baby has also become quite noisy. Next to mouthing, he loves banging. A real tambourine is a great toy. So are aluminum pie plates, spoons, and cups banged on the floor or high-chair tray. This baby is beginning to be a tool user.

8–12 Months: Exploration

For the first time in the baby's life, his environment is accessible. He can get anywhere he sees and wants to go. And he is curious. He'll explore the electrical cords and outlets; he'll figure out how to open kitchen cabinets; he'll eventually pull himself up and pull things off the coffee table. This is the time to babyproof the house, because the baby's agility and ability will make *everything* accessible. And he doesn't understand "NO." Even a pin on the floor, bits of fluff or pills can be popped in the mouth with that increasingly accurate pincer grasp. Very few commercial toys are necessary for children at this stage because the environment is the toy. Obviously, close supervision is essential.

Because this is the age of exploration, the baby will enjoy exploring busy boxes when he's confined in the crib, playpen or high chair. There are many interesting **Busy Boxes** detailed in this book.

A new skill the baby develops in this period is the deliberate release of grasp. Up until about 8 or 9 months old, the baby either let go of something unintentionally or let go when something more appealing was presented. Now, however, the baby can let go at will. He'll drop toys from his high chair tray, jars of food from the shopping cart, sponges out of the bath. It is an exciting skill to the baby and he will practice it and practice it.

Babies of this age enjoy taking things out of containers—a coffee can or plastic canister can be filled with interesting household objects: empty spools, spray-can lids, a string of measuring spoons, a nylon scrubber—anything that is of a safe size and interesting texture. **In and Out** toys are fun now.

Because the baby can crawl well by this stage, he will enjoy crawling after balls, and playing roly-poly games with Mom and Dad. An assortment of interesting **Balls** add to the fun.

The 8–12 month baby is very clingy to his parents, possibly even crying about the short separation when Mom has to go to the bathroom. Outside, with strangers, the baby is *very* shy and very reluctant to be handled. This is part of the object/people permanence concept. Prior to this the baby has been uncertain (and uninterested) about what happens to things he can't see. For all he knows and cares, a person leaving a room ceases to exist. A toy dropped on the floor disappears. At about 8 months, however, the baby begins to realize that life isn't quite that drastic. He begins to look for the dropped object and to wonder about where Mom is. A fun game is peek-a-boo with people and objects. Partially cover a toy loosely with a cloth and let the baby find it. Loosely cover your face with a cloth and let the baby find you.

The baby at this stage is truly on his way to being a tool user. With glee he pounds and bangs anything and everything together, understanding the rather subtle concept that using one object to bang another object causes something to happen. There are some wonderful toys for this. Some of the **Musical Toys** are especially fun.

12–24 Months: Active

The 1–2 year old is rarely still. He can walk and will. He can climb and does. This stage has many falls and many cuddles from Mom or Dad. The baby's physical abilities far exceed his mental capacity for prethought. He simply isn't able to foresee the consequences of his actions—each time he does something it's as if he does it for the first time. If he throws a cup down the stairs and it breaks, it doesn't occur to him that another cup would break if thrown or that his mom might again scold him. He doesn't remember; he can't predict.

He is intensely curious, and his increasing physical skills mean that the whole world is his playground. The parents can get quite despairing during this active stage, wondering if there will ever again be a time their baby will sit quietly, intent on less active pursuits. The parent must understand that for this year, the child *needs* to move and play. There will be quiet times but they will be brief.

Clearly all this progress takes practice, and practice is what we need to encourage. Active toys are appropriate for this stage. Many of the **Gross Motor** toys are ideal for a child this age.

Another major change in the baby during his second year is his increasing ability to imitate. He'll pick up anything resembling a cup, be it spray-can lid or flowerpot, and pretend to drink from it. He'll pick up a comb and comb his teddy bear's fur. This will evolve into brief games of imitative play, where the child is actually inventing the form of the play. This kind of play will undergo further evolution as the child enters his third year. Toys for imitative play during the second year are based on the child's experience level—they will primarily be home-based toys. Some of the beginning toys for **Creative Play** will be fun.

When the 1–2 year old can be persuaded to sit and play with toys, the toys must be engaging enough to keep him interested. His hand skills are quite developed by this stage, but unless the toy is very interesting, the baby will quickly move on to somethig that is. **Musical Toys** are especially interesting. There are a number of **Fine Motor Toys** detailed in this book that are intriguing even to a busy 1 year old.

Books are another way to engage the child of this age. Nothing is as warmly close as a parent and child sitting together looking at books. Sturdy books with cardboard pages are interesting toys to the young child, because like magic, the picture changes with every turn. There are many many books available with a clear one-picture-per-page format. The child will recognize the pictures as being something *he* knows.

2–3 Years: Ordering His Life: Manipulation of Things and People

By the time of the second birthday, parents tend to think of their child as a child, not as a baby. Physically, the child is very well developed.

He has made tremendous progress in gross motor skills in these two years. He can lift, carry, climb, leap, run, kick, throw, and even clumsily catch a ball. Having accomplished many of these feats during his second year, he doesn't have quite the drive to be in a state of perpetual motion as he had in the year just past.

This is the age of the educational toy. Sorting by shape and size, picture matching, puzzles, even some color matching are all interesting to the child of this age. **Shape Sorting Boxes, Piling/ Nesting Toys, Threading Toys,** and **Two Handed Toys** will all be used over and over again.

Puzzles too are exciting for a 2 year old. Most will be able to do only the formboard-style puzzles with one puzzle piece per hole. There are many of these puzzles on the market. Children love the peek-in ones with a picture underneath each piece. By the end of the year many children will be able to master 5–10 piece inlaid puzzles. Many interesting **Puzzles** are detailed in this book.

Some of the early lotto type games can be used with the 2 year old for picture matching. Although he won't have any interest at all in playing Lotto or Memory as games, he will be intrigued by finding pictures that match. Look at **Language Play** for enriching this development.

Parents and educators must take care, however, not to overemphasize the importance of all these educational toys. Yes, the child enjoys them and yes, they are important for his development, but they are limited toys. The child needs plenty of opportunity to play with less goal-oriented toys. The child's ability to play imaginatively is also developing, and while it isn't the passion it will be at age three and onwards, it needs equal time to give it a chance to develop. The 2 year old, already able to imitate real life in his play with sink sets and tea sets, now becomes able to abstract even further. He'll understand that a small piece of plastic with foam rubber on it is a bed, and that a little plastic semicircle with the depression in the middle is a chair and these little cylinders with a bead on top are people. And while his play won't be richly imaginative because of his language limitations, he'll enjoy putting the people in bed and in the chairs. These **Creative Play** toys will be enjoyed for years, as the child's ability to imagine develops more and more.

Play with other children at this age is difficult at best. The 2 year old has no concept of sharing or of ownership. It is the era of "I see, I want, I take." Mothers try valiantly to put together play groups for their 2 year olds, but these get-togethers are usually fraught with tears as one child grabs the other child's favorite car and is then pushed down by a third child who is in turn hit by a fourth child. Outdoor play, as long as each child has a bike and each child has a sand shovel so they don't need to battle, is usually more successful.

The child who enjoyed picture books as a 1 year old will now begin to enjoy books with a simple story line. Even some of the more involved folk tales may have enough repetition to keep a 2–3 year old engrossed.

3–5 Years: Imagination and Socialization

The 3- to 5-year old child has rather amazing skills. His large movements have the precision and grace we associate with mature control. His hand control is fine enough to draw and cut. Socially, he has learned many of the rules of his society and he is eager to spend time with his peers. Emotionally, he has developed foresight (and its accompanying worries) and compassion. Cognitively, he is able to abstract.

Provision of play materials for children of this age includes provision of playmates. Almost everything a child enjoys doing at this age he enjoys even more in the company of his peers, so most children this age will enjoy attending preschool.

For large muscle play, playground equipment is just right. Three, 4, and 5 year olds love climbing apparatus, the large slides and learning how to pump the swings. Jumping on an old mattress is also great fun, especially if they can jump down on it from a fairly high object. The fearless abandon of the two year old has been replaced by caution and a fairly good sense of what might be safe, what might be too high and what might be too fast. A homemade obstacle course that gives the child opportunities to run, jump, crawl, and climb over, under, and through is a wonderful adventure.

Indoor play revolves around one goal—creating. The child has a high interest in fine motor activities: clay, dough, blocks, beads, puzzles, as well as scissors, paper, collage materials and glue are all used with precision to create *something*. Children this age love building with blocks—either wooden or snap-together—and will spend a long time building houses or cars or space stations. The keen observer will see how different this goal-oriented building is from the random stacking done by the 2 year old. Attribute this to two big cognitive changes: the ability to abstract and the ability to plan. He can look at a red plastic rectangle with six bumps on top and draw mental pictures of a finished product: "If I add wheels, this will be a car; if I make a row of them, it will be a wall." Working with playdough and an assortment of tools to cut, pound, poke, and shape also is a favorite activity. While the 2 year old will enjoy simply squeezing the dough, the 3 or 4 year old will make tacos or pizza or birthday cake.

The hallmark of the 3–5 year old is this imagination, and its expression is most dramatic during make-believe play. A group of four year olds in a preschool will have an ongoing drama complete with costumes, names and a script dictated on the spot. "I'm the mother and you're the father and he's the baby and you have to go get the babysitter but she's sick." Make-believe play gives the child an opportunity to experiment with the roles and rules of his culture, to play at problem solving and handling power, sharing and taking turns. Adults need to provide the basics for this play—the space, the playthings and the playmates. Essential equipment is an assortment of hats, some cast-off adult clothing with enough tucks and hems so that the child isn't always falling, adult shoes, and plenty of jewelry. For the 3 and 4 year olds the more glittery this clothing is the better they like it! Garage and rummage sales are the best places to find great items like purple satin formals and silver high heels.

A supply of plastic food and an assortment of salvaged "real" containers like egg boxes, cereal boxes, coffee cans, and the like help the child cook wonderful imaginary meals.

Other imaginative playthings needed for childen of this age are a medical kit, a cash register, an assortment of cars and trucks, and blocks of several kinds. The snap together blocks are wonderful, but very different in feel and play ability from the traditional wooden blocks. Children appreciate access to both.

Of course the child doesn't spend all his time in imaginative play. There are many excellent skill oriented toys that he will greatly enjoy, particularly during times that he has no peers to play with. **Construction Toys, Design and Pattern Sets, Listening Games, Puzzles,** and some **Language Games** will add to enjoyment and fun.

The 4 or 5 year old has at least an awareness of number, and there are some good early **Number Materials** available from educational suppliers.

By the age of four children are interested in beginning board games. Many of them may still find losing very difficult, but the game rules and waiting for a turn appeals to the child's sense of order and fair play. The **Games** section details a number of good games for beginners.

The School Age Child: Learning His Role in Society

The play of the school age child is very sophisticated. Gross and fine motor skills are well established. The child's focus now centers on perfecting his understanding of the roles and rules of society.

For the first time, sex makes a difference in the child's play time. Be it nature or nurture, most school age boys will choose karate over ballet; most school age girls will play dolls rather than Star Wars. Boys will join the hockey team; girls will join the gymnastics club. Boys will build model airplanes; girls will make potholders. Indeed, grade school age boys and girls show a distinct aversion to children of the opposite sex. A boy and girl who were best of friends during preschool and kindergarten now draw away from each other. If they do retain contact, it is done at home, away from taunting peers. Because the focus of this age group is on learning to fit into the larger society, boys learn how to be boys from boys; girls learn from girls.

Team sports, organized instruction in music, art and drama, and elaborate games of make-believe occupy the child's out-of-school hours. Many children are involved in after-school lessons and activities three, four, or even five days a week, with additional lessons on Saturday. There is hardly any time left for the child to just be with friends or play on his own.

Nevertheless, children need a good amount of free time. Unstructured time not only gives the child an opportunity to draw on his own inventive resources, but it also gives him a measure of control over his own life as he decides how to spend this time.

Playthings for the school age child are mostly those seen on television advertising. No longer can the parent simply buy a doll for the child. Rather, she must buy the doll that walks on its tippytoes, says "More please," chews its food and burps when it is patted. Boys aren't satisfied with just a car. Instead, they need the black Trans Am with lighted headlights, three speeds, and a door panel that can be flipped to show a dent after a crash. Less imagination is required of the child. Much of the playability of the toy is dictated by the manufacturers. But once the gimmicks have been explored, the child probably will play with the toy the way children have always played: the doll will be loved and fed and changed and spanked; the car will be pushed along the floor, scratched along the furniture, and garaged in an empty shoebox.

The single most valuable toy for a young school age child—boy or girl—is a doll's house. Children from 5 to 9 years old have a wonderful time with a doll house. It is a manageable environment. Even if boys use Star Wars' people and girls use Strawberry Shortcake miniatures, a doll house lets them create a miniuniverse where *they* are in control. A doll house will enable the child to play through some of the worries, mysteries, and joys of life on a scale and intensity decided upon and controlled by the child. This is what play for this age group is all about.

INFANT STIMULATION

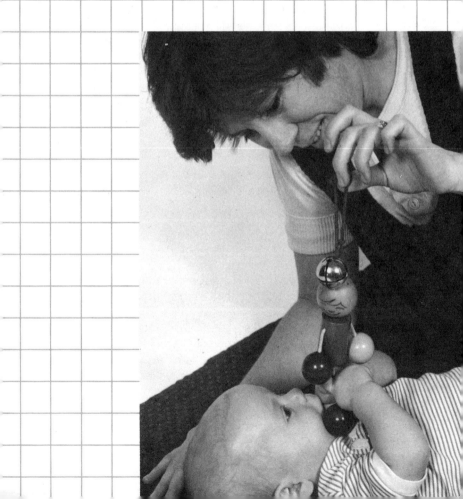

INFANT STIMULATION
TOYS TO LOOK AT

The newborn has two basic play skills from the time he comes home from the hospital: he can look and he can hear. At first his vision is accurate for a distance of only about six inches, so whatever he's given to look at should be put close to his face. His hearing is very sensitive. The "startle" reflex is still present, so sounds should be mellow, not sudden or sharp. During the very early weeks the main emphasis of both parent and child will be getting enough sleep, getting enough to eat, keeping warm, and getting to know each other. At about 6 weeks, however, the baby settles: the parent starts to know who this little person is, what he likes and dislikes, when he's likely to want to sleep and eat and be awake. The baby begins to have longer periods awake and has learned that his cries will be heard and taken care of. Life becomes calmer, if not easier, for both parent and child.

During this period of adjustment, life itself is enough stimulation for the baby, and the parents' voices and faces the best possible playthings. Nothing extra is needed, because every thing and every place is new territory to be explored with all his senses. Everything is a sensory bombardment to this new little human.

But after the settling period, it is appropriate to begin adding stimulation. Pictures can be propped in the side of the crib for the baby to look at when lying on his back or stomach. Commercial mobiles can be hung where the baby will see them. It's probably too soon to hang a mobile from the crib because the baby won't be able to get his head in a position to see it. But hang a mobile or anything else brightly colored in the area where the baby sits in his infant seat. It might be good to install right-angle plant-hanging brackets in one or two places around the house so that pretty things can be hung for the baby while he's seated.

This is a time for parents to think of and make things to hang for their baby. Because the tiny baby isn't yet using his hands with any accuracy, even objects like feathers, colored foil, wrapping paper, and ribbons are safe to hang within seeing distance. The book *Smart Toys* by Burtt and Kalkstein is a very rich resource for this and later stages.

A huge variety of mobiles is available commercially. Consider, though, when choosing a mobile, that the colors should be bright. Babies don't see pastels as easily as they see bright primary colors. Also make sure that the colors are bright underneath, from the baby's point of view.

Color Mobile

The startlingly bright geometrics of this mobile will be fascinating for a tiny baby to gaze at. Even a child with some degree of visual impairment will be able to see the contrasts of the bright colors and the bold lines. Because Color Mobile makes no sound, it is most appropriate for the very early months when gazing, rather than batting, is the baby's best skill.
Semper/2/*Price Code A*

Fisher-Price Dancing Animals Music Box Mobile

The music box on this mobile plays for 10 minutes, long enough to soothe even an extremely resistant baby. The colorful animals and flowers can be detached, allowing for parental creativity in hanging new things so the baby doesn't get bored.
Fisher-Price/1/*Price Code A*

Crib Activity Arch

This beautiful soft sculpture crib gym/mobile is made of colorful fabric, and attaches to the sides of the crib with Velcro straps. Two brightly colored soft-bodied toys which attach to the arch are included.
Johnson & Johnson/1/*Price Code B*

Carousel

The carousel music box is uniquely adaptable. Bright primary colored animals revolve as the music plays. The carousel can be attached to the top of the crib or playpen, hung on the wall, or put onto the pedestal base for use on the floor. Hardware for all three positions is included. The music box is turned on by pulling a string, which an adult will have to do. As the baby gets older, enjoyment will be had from batting and pushing at the animals as they glide by.

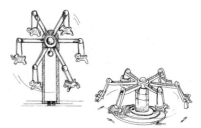

Berchet/2/*Price Code C*

Octopus Music Box

This is probably the earliest active music toy. While the young baby doesn't cause the music to happen by his activity, the toy invites active response. Brightly colored 1¼" wooden balls are attached to the music box on tight springs. Even a gentle or random hand motion will get the balls clacking together. The balls and springs rotate as the music plays and this, too, causes interesting motion. This is a beautiful toy. It is fairly delicate, though, as are most music boxes, so it shouldn't be offered to a baby with enough strength and control to pick it up by one of the balls and throw it across the room.

Kouvalias/2/*Price Code D*

TOYS TO BAT AT

The tiny baby will spend part of her day lying on her back. Her movements will be large and uncontrolled, both arms and legs involved in random movement. Although this movement is random, it can be capitalized on by placing easy action/easy response floor and hanging toys within reach of those waving arms. Although it may seem at first to be accidental that the baby has hit the toy, the parent will quickly realize that it's happening too frequently to be purely accidental. The baby has seen the target, has learned what happens when it's touched, and has deliberately repeated the action. What an accomplishment!

FOR THE FLOOR

Happy Apple
A bright clear red, the Happy Apple has a mellow chime inside that rings as the apple tips and rights itself. The bright color is an instant attention-getter.
Fisher-Price/1/*Price Code A*

Chime Bird

This roly-poly bird tips and rights itself when even gently pushed. Its chime is louder than most roly-polys, but not loud enough to be startling. Although a tiny baby won't recognize it as a bird, the clear, bright blue of the base will attract attention.
Playskool/1/*Price Code A*

Chime Ball

Small rocking animals are visible through the see-through top of this classic chiming roly-poly toy. A gentle push causes the ball to wobble and the chime to ring.
Fisher-Price/1/*Price Code A*

Rolling Mirror

This mirror on wheels looks like an enlarged parakeet toy. The mirror is suspended between two large wheels and its angle is just right for looking into while lying on the floor, either supine or prone. The wheels have spokes large enough for a little hand to grasp to move the mirror back and forth.
Semper/2/*Price Code B*

Turn and Learn Activity Center

The Lazy Susan bottom on this activity center makes it easy for even random movement to cause the toy to spin. Each of the four sides has a separate activity—a clicking dial, a rabbit on a spring, three beads to slide, and an unbreakable mirror. At first the baby will delight in just getting the activity center spinning; later she will begin to explore the possibilities of each side. Still later, she may be able to squeak the squeaker on top, so this is a toy that is interesting for quite a while.

Fisher-Price/1/*Price Code B*

Aqua Toy

This see-through cylinder is partially filled with water, where two little plastic fish swim in full view. When the cylinder is pushed, the water sloshes and the fish clack against the sides. An exciting variation for using this toy was devised by a parent of a baby with visual and hearing impairment: she chilled the Aqua Toy in the refrigerator, and later warmed it in hot water so that it became a tactile stimulus.

Ambi/2/*Price Code B*

TO HANG

Bouncing Cradle

Positioning a tiny baby for play can
sometimes be difficult because she
does not have the strength to hold
her head up for long when prone,
and cannot hold her head in midline
when supine. This cloth chair
provides just the right amount of
support to enable the baby to
comfortably look and play. The
extended foot plate enables the
baby to provide her own movement
as her heels kick. A snap-on toy bar
is also available. It must be ordered
from England.
Mothercare/3/*Price Code C*

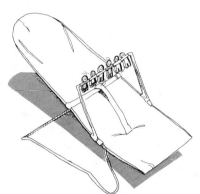

Air Chair

This chair, available from an American firm, is very similar to the chair
described above. The main difference is that instead of cloth, a wipe-
clean vinyl mesh fabric is used, and there is no toy bar available.
Community Playthings/3/*Price Code D*

Toy Rods

For hanging toys, so they can be batted at, three different styles of
toy rod are available: a straight wooden rod sized to go across a crib, a
right angle rod adjustable in height for attaching to either crib or
playpen, and a simple rod with webbing straps that can be put across
crib or playpen.

Laplandia/2/*Crib toy rod:*   *Price Code B*
L-bow rod: *Price Code B*
Simple toy rod: *Price Code A*

Portaplay Gym

This free-standing, lightweight frame is designed to hold hanging toys from its adjustable Velcro straps. The baby can be placed on the floor under the frame or seated in his infant chair under the frame or the frame can be placed in the crib. Ideal also for therapeutic uses. It's like giving the therapist an extra hand for holding enticing toys while she/he concentrates on the child.
Portaplay Toys/3/*Price Code B*

Rooster Bell Toy

Primary colored wooden dowels hang from the top of this batting toy. As the baby's arm swipes across the dowels, a very pleasing wind-chime sound is produced. As the baby's hands get more skillful, he'll grab and shake the dowels, making quite a clatter!
Schowanek/2/*Price Code B*

Bell Ringer

The white-painted bells ring loud and clearly. Wooden beads hang down low enough for even random arm movement to cause the bells to ring. As the baby's skills develop, he'll grab the beads and pull and shake so that it's *really* noisy. Many parents find that it's a little *too* noisy first thing in the morning.
Laplandia/2/*Price Code B*

Jonny Bell

The big wooden beads on this hanging man invite a baby to touch and pull. A large jingle bell makes great noise, the hardwood beads clack together and because the whole toy is suspended from heavy elastic, there's great action when it's pulled and released. Expensive, but of exceptional quality.
Schowanek/2/*Price Code B*

Jingle Duck

This bright yellow duck is suspended from heavy elastic. A large jingle bell hangs inside his body and the toy is easy to grasp, shake, and ring.
Schowanek/2/*(Kaplan)Price Code A*

Little Guys

A variety of brightly colored wooden beads and brass rings hangs from an elastic cord. When batted it makes a very mellow sound.
Laplandia/2/*Price Code A*

Pop Top

Pull the string hanging below this geometric target and up pops a fuzzy-haired face. Great peek-a-boo game.
Laplandia/2/*Price Code B*

Pendulum Kicker

The baby's hitting and kicking skills have to be quite advanced to zero in on this little target, but the spinning action and ringing bell are great rewards.

Laplandia/2/*Price Code A*

TO GRASP AND HANDLE

Once the baby has had plenty of practice batting at things, he will begin to spend time looking at his hands, following their movement from side to middle, up and over. He'll bring his hands together and watch that happen, looking from one hand to the other as the distance narrows. This is all part of eye/hand coordination. The baby is learning where his hands are, and how they can be used. He will reach for an object and sometimes be able to grasp it. This is the golden age for rattles, because as soon as he's able to consistently grasp the rattle, he'll begin active exploration, first bringing it to his mouth, then shaking it, and later examining it with his eyes and transferring the toy from hand to hand.

Wrist Rattles

These brightly colored cloth animal faces have a rattle inside and a band that easily fastens with Velcro to a baby's wrist or ankle. Wearing these rattles, a baby can get added pleasure from waving hands or feet.
Fisher-Price/1/*Price Code A*

Red Rings

This red rattle looks like a planet surrounded by rings, an orbiting satellite attached to the center with flexible plastic. The red rings are made of a very grippable plastic; it almost seems to stick onto the baby's hand, making for very successful grasping. The bright color, mellow bell sound, and random movement of the "satellite" all make this an intriguing first rattle. The circumference of the rings is so small and the whole rattle is so light that even babies who were preemies can use it.
Johnson & Johnson/1/*Price Code A*

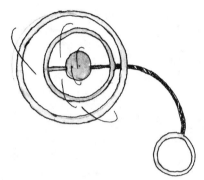

Dumbell Rattles

These rattles come in pairs, and are a perfect size and weight for small babies. With one red rattle and one blue, the baby will do lots of visual comparing. It's unusual for rattles to come in pairs, yet how logical: handedness certainly isn't established at 3 to 6 months, so we want the baby to use and explore using *both* hands. Reasonably priced, too.
Kiddicraft/2/*Price Code A*

Rumba Safety Rattle

Although this rattle has to be ordered from England, it is worth it. Dumbell shaped, it is extremely lightweight and fits into a baby's grasp perfectly. Even the slightest movement produces a rewarding clatter. An ideal early rattle.

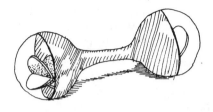

Mothercare/3/*Price Code A*

Ball Rattle

Brightly-colored 1¼" plastic balls are threaded on stout cord with a teething ring on the end. The balls have rattles inside. Even tiny fingers find it easy to get a hold on the cord and wave this colorful sound-maker around. This toy can also be hung by putting a toy rod through the teething ring.

Ambi/2/*Price Code A*

Ring Rattle

Circular rattles are the easiest rattles for a baby who is just beginning to work on hand-to-hand transfer. This rattle has several features that make it a favorite: the clear plastic ring is a perfect size for a baby's grasp, the noise made by the beads inside the ring is easy to produce, and there is visual interest in tracking the beads as they whiz around the circle.

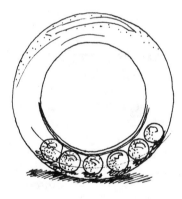

Kiddicraft/2/*Price Code A*

Double Circle Rattle

This rattle is the ultimate in simplicity of design. Two hardwood circles, one red, one natural wood color, are linked. That's all. But if you shake it, the circles click against each other. If it's put in the mouth, it's very satisfying because the edges are square and that makes for great gum massage. Because of the two rings, babies often bring both hands to the middle to play with it. A great toy.

Schowanek/2/*Price Code A*

Helicopter Rattle

This lightweight rattle has lots of different places to hold on to, making hand-to-hand transfer easy. Color-contrasting parts of the helicopter move. Sometimes a baby will hold the toy with one hand while spinning these parts with the other.
Discovery/3/*Price Code A*

Red Ball in Wood Circle

Inside this simple wooden ring is a crossbar with a bright red ball that clacks from side to side when shaken. The edges of the ring are square, so mouthing is interesting.
Schowanek/2/*Price Code A*

Four-Ring Rattle

This unusual rattle is a vinyl tube with variously textured rings and beads hanging from it. Babies love the noise the brass ring makes, and love chewing on the rubber ring.
Laplandia/2/*Price Code A*

Teething Ring

This vinyl tube circle has beads of different shapes, textures, and sizes attached to it. Great for mouthing and shaking.
Laplandia/2/*Price Code A*

Slinky

An old favorite has been brought back in plastic. Available in an array of bright colors, this toy is terrific for even small babies to play with. By catching a hand at each end of the Slinky, the baby becomes aware of the possibilities of *two-handed* play.

James Industries/1/*Price Code A*

Active Baby

This set of four brightly colored toys can be used for a long time, because so many different kinds of play are possible. The rattle-roller, push-squeaker, cone-whistle, and mirror-cube can be used individually by the young baby, or piled into a tower by the older child.

Ambi/2/*Price Code B*

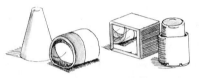

Music Box Teddy Bear

Although this toy is designed to be hung from crib or playpen, it is equally good as a parent-held toy. An easily pulled brightly colored handle hangs from the plastic teddy bear. When pulled and released, the music box plays. Because the music doesn't start to play until the handle is released, this toy helps teach a baby about releasing his grasp.

Fisher-Price/1/*Price Code A*

Latex Menagerie

Babies delight in the sound of squeaky toys. Many squeaky toys, however, are made of material that is just too rigid for a baby's tiny hands to manage squeezing. Latex squeeze toys are so soft that just the act of picking them up causes a little squeak. The baby will figure out all sorts of ways to produce sound—chewing on it, using two hands on it, tapping it against the floor, the knee, the head. Additionally, they are available in many shapes and bright colors *and* with some wonderful textures.
Marlon/2/*for 1 Price Code B*

Wiggle Worm

Many handling activities are possible with this unusual textural toy. There are numerous places to grasp, so hand-to-hand transfer is easy. Textures inside the fabric head, body, and tail can be explored by squeezing. Rubbery rings are flexible and just right for mouth exploration. The whole toy is machine washable.
Johnson & Johnson/1/*Price Code B*

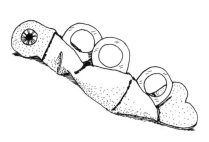

BALLS

Few toys are as engaging as balls. For the almost-crawling child, a ball is enticingly out of reach, moving on a bit as soon as touched by the child. As an interactive toy, a ball is wonderful. One person pushes it and the other person pushes it back. Very little physical skill is required to push a smoothly rolling ball, and a ball can be played with in all positions: side-lying, prone, supine, sitting or standing. A game of ball can be an ideal way to make contact with a shy child, as fears dissolve with the simple joy of pushing a ball back and forth.

Water Mates

This small see-through plastic ball has a duck floating in the water inside it. As the ball rolls, the water sloshes from side to side and the duck taps against the sides. The weight of the water makes this ball heavier than the baby has learned to expect, so it's a very interesting toy to reach for. Additional tactile interest can be added by putting the ball in the refrigerator. As it's small enough to be played with on the tummy while the baby lies supine, he can really feel the difference in temperature.

Kiddicraft/2/*Price Code A*

Li'l Bubble Ball

As the ball rolls, three animals twirl up and down a central post inside this see-through ball. The movement is fascinating. Fun in the bathtub, too.

Tomy/1/*Price Code A*

Rock and Roll Ball

This bright red ball is made of rigid plastic. A smaller ball is inset into its circumference, and spins when the ball is pushed. Rock and Roll Ball rattles, too!
Ambi/2/*Price Code A*

Discovery Ball

An "hourglass" with small beads that clatter through as the ball rolls or is shaken makes this ball special. In addition, the slotted sides of the sphere make it easy for most children to hold on.
Battat/2/*Price Code A*

Pull Apart Ball

This ball is made of soft, chewable rubber. It is easy for small hands to get a strong grasp on the interlocking rings. Because the ball doesn't roll very far when pushed, it's ideal for the newly crawling child.
International Playthings/2/*Price Code A*

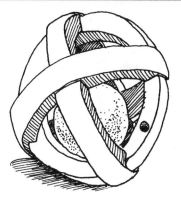

SUCTION TOYS

Suction toys are designed to stick to a smooth surface, anchoring them while the child plays. In practice, however, the suction doesn't last long, and often isn't strong enough to withstand the pushing and pulling a baby gives it. But if it is fastened to the side or floor of the bathtub, a suction toy will stick very well on the cold damp enamel, and becomes a nonsinking bath toy. Outside the bath, these toys work well if the parent holds the base while the child plays. This gives the child the option of extending the play by picking the toy up, shaking it, and chewing on the rubber suction base.

Rota Rattle

As the baby spins the rotating arms on this suction toy, the rings slide up and down, making a mellow rattling sound. The bright primary colors are very attractive, and the action of this toy calls for more hand and finger involvement than most suction toys.
Ambi/2/*Price Code A*

Spinning Butterfly

The see-through plastic top on this suction toy encloses a butterfly with mirror-like reflectors and several rattling beads.
Fisher-Price/1/*Price Code A*

Wobble Globe

Three bright, lightweight balls bounce and rattle inside the see-through globe. The rubber suction foot is good to chew on when it's not attached to a surface. A nice play variation is possible with this toy: the see-through globe can be unscrewed and partially filled with water. It is remarkable how the extra weight changes the movement and sound of this toy.

Kiddicraft/2/*Price Code A*

Squeak and Peek Sailor

Quite a few play variations are possible with this toy. The sailor rattles when pushed over and bounces back, the squeaker on top produces quite a good sound, and the little man's arms can be raised over his face for a game of peek-a-boo.

Fisher-Price/1/*Price Code A*

Pull-up Pets

Three brightly colored molded plastic animals sit on top of the base of this suction toy. A large handle attached to a string is pulled to make the animals stand up, and it is noisy fun to knock them down and start all over again. The oversized suction cup sticks exceptionally well.

Playskool/1/*Price Code A*

Stand-up Man

This suction toy is unusual. A three-sided little man with a sturdy pull string and ring gets pulled to stand on top of the suction base. It's great fun to knock him down and pull him up again. The rather sophisticated concept of cause and effect is involved here.

Johnson & Johnson/1/*Price Code A*

PULL TOYS

Although pull toys are usually used by toddlers to pull behind them while walking, they also make a good floor toy for a baby. At first they can be used for tracking, with the parent pulling the toy and the baby following the path of the toy with her eyes. Later, when she can sit up, the baby can be given the string and can pull the toy toward her. Understanding the cause and effect relationship of this is a great cognitive accomplishment for the baby. She has learned that if she wants to get the toy closer to her, she has to pull the string. Of course, for her to *want* the toy closer to her, it must be an interesting toy. These are.

Queen Buzzy Bee

The bright orange wings on this wooden bee whirl and the spring antennae quiver as this small toy is pulled. A gentle sound accompanies the action. The baby will love bouncing the antennae once the toy is close.
Fisher-Price/1/*Price Code A*

Troller

Children of all ages are fascinated by this toy. The bright colors and geometrics of the balls are very beautiful to watch as they turn and roll. The sound it makes is very gentle, so it won't be frightening to a child who still startles easily. For the walking child it has the great quality of never tipping over!
Small World Toys/2/*Price Code A*

Rhythm Rollers

This bright red truck holds three sound cylinders that clatter as the string is pulled. Once the baby gets the truck, he can take the cylinders out, shake them, roll them, and try to put them back.

Johnson & Johnson/1/*Price Code A*

Little Snoopy

This wooden dog has a spring tail and ears that can be flipped around. A barking sound accompanies the movement. Babies love playing with the springy tail and surprisingly enough also enjoy flipping and spinning the ears.

Fisher-Price/1/*Price Code A*

Flying Octopus

Bright primary colored wooden balls are attached to the body of this toy on tight springs. As the toy is pulled, the balls and springs turn, creating great visual interest. Children delight in flipping and clacking the balls.

Kouvalias/2/*Price Code C*

FINE MOTOR

FINE MOTOR/ VISUAL PERCEPTION TOYS

Fine motor control begins when a child is still a baby. The progression of hand gazing, hands to mouth, batting at toys, and grasping at rattles lays the foundation for fine motor control, as the baby learns where his hands are in space and begins to practice control over what those hands can do. Practice is the key word in achieving the delicate and precise movements we think of as fine motor control. Just as an adult must practice a golf swing, needlepoint stitches, or tennis serves to achieve precise control, a child must practice his hand movements to achieve accuracy.

Often the practice during the baby stages of fine motor control goes unnoticed. But by the time the baby is in a high chair and practicing grasp release by continually dropping food over the side of the tray, tossing toys out of the crib or carriage, or flinging jars of baby food out of the shopping cart, people notice.

This evolution from crude hand movements to fine hand movements takes a lot of practice!

A nonhandicapped child will practice on whatever toys or nontoys are in her environment, constantly seeking out a challenge and staying with it until it is easy. Pegboards, television knobs, sorting boxes, kitchen cabinets, beads and laces, screw tops—all are grist for the churning mill we call a child. A handicapped child, however, may be only too content to stay in one place and bang a rattle or watch his hands. Adults must attract his attention to new possibilities and challenges. It is through toys that adults can capture the child's attention and help bring about, however gradually, a controlled series of challenges.

BUSY BOXES

A busy box is a convenient way for a confined baby to do some exploring. With the box attached to the side of crib or playpen, or placed on a high-chair tray, the baby will delight in pushing, poking, spinning and pulling the various activity areas, learning about cause and effect.

A child with normal mobility will swing kitchen cabinets back and forth, take the lids off pans, move on to poking things under the refrigerator, and then zip out and fiddle with the electric cords. It is a time of constant motion, constant exploration. The physically impaired child doesn't have this freedom of movement, but may well have the same curiosity. For the baby and young child whose mobility is limited by physical impairment, busy boxes are sometimes one of the only ways exploration is possible.

Fold 'n' Go Activity Quilt

This playmat gives tactile stimulation as well as providing activities to keep a baby amused. Made of brightly colored machine-washable fabric, the activities are all located at one end of the mat. The baby can lay on the mat and play with the activities. A mirror is revealed by picking up a colorful flap, a little cloth rabbit can be put into a pocket or fed with a crinkly sounding carrot, and a furry nest is home for a chewable plastic bird.
Playskool/1/*Price Code C*

Spin 'n' Roll Rattles

Four see-through cylinders are mounted on the base of this unusual busy box. The inside of each cylinder is different, visually attractive, and makes a sound. A simple batting motion causes a cylinder to spin, thus activating the colorful contents.
Battat/2/*Price Code B*

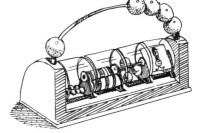

Barnyard Sights and Sounds

Bright graphics illustrate the barnyard scene on this fabric activity center. Next to each adult animal pictured on the playmat is a flap, and a game of peek-a-boo reveals the baby animal hiding underneath. The playmat can be tied onto the side of a crib or playpen, or played with on the floor.

Johnson & Johnson/1/*Price Code B*

Activity Center

This free-standing busy box has several activity areas: A chiming cylinder with simple pictures on it, an easily squeaked dog face, a brightly colored flower-shaped cylinder that rattles when it spins, a bell to ring, a ratchet-sounding handle to push and pull back and forth, and brightly colored beads to push back and forth. All are contained in a nicely weighted box that is just the right depth for a young child.

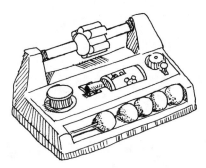

Battat/2/*Price Code B*

Peek-A-Boo Doors

This wedge-shaped activity center has four doors to open in order to discover a hidden activity inside. Each door opens differently. The activities are interesting but not difficult. Children enjoy the surprise of discovering what's behind each door.

Battat/2/*Price Code B*

Seaside Activity Center

A great deal of language play is possible with this busy box. The activity areas have been integrated into a seaside scene, so it is possible to talk about the picture as a whole as the little girl's inner tube is squeezed or the beach ball is spun or the sailboat is rocked.
Kiddicraft/2/*Price Code B*

Air Pressure Activity Center

Squeezing and releasing causes amazing things to happen on this busy box. Free-standing, there are three activity areas on this box. Squeezing one of the rubber buttons causes tiny brightly colored balls to hop around inside a see-through plastic globe. By squeezing the other button, tiny brightly colored plastic balls are sent through a see-through maze. The third activity requires pushing and pulling. A pull on the handle causes two beads to shoot across see-through tubes at the front of the box.
Battat/2/*Price Code C*

Busy Poppin Pals

Few toys are as surprising to the young child as this one. Five Disney characters pop up from behind closed lids as a variety of switches are operated. One switch resembles a light switch, one is a push-button, another slides back and forth, a telephone dial triggers another. Children enjoy the challenge of operating the switches, the surprise of seeing the character pop up, *and* the job of pushing the lids closed.
Gabriel/1/*Price Code B*

Action Activity Center Pop-ups

The height of this box may make it necessary for an adult to help stabilize it so it doesn't tip onto the child, but the activities are so interesting that it's worth having anyway. Banging on one button causes a little bird to travel up a post, and then "peck" his way down. Another button causes a ball to shoot up to the top of a post and hit a sun face, which then spins. A dial (quite difficult to turn) causes a bell to ring. By reaching up to the top of Hand-Pops the child can twist a ratchet-sounding airplane and ring the bell.
Battat/2/*Price Code C*

IN AND OUT TOYS

The concept of in and out can begin being taught before the child has the manual dexterity to do pegboards. The skill prerequisite is that the child has developed a grasp release.

Three Men in a Tub

This is an ideal toy for teaching in and out. Brightly colored plastic, the tub is about 7 inches across, with a chiming, weighted base. The three men are also weighted at the bottom and each has a differently shaped hat for grasping. Success at getting the man out is usually accompanied by the chime ringing, and success at putting them in is almost guaranteed, because the tub is so open and so much larger than the men.
Fisher-Price/1/*Price Code A*

Balls in a Bowl

A transparent yellow plastic fishbowl with three transparent balls, each with a colorful spinner inside. The balls are often too big for a young child to grasp, but smaller or more graspable objects can be substituted. The fishbowl is terrific used in conjunction with any objects because the object is still visible even though it's inside the bowl.
Johnson & Johnson/1/*Price Code B*

Wobbly Colors

This brightly colored plastic toy has several uses. Four small balls fit into a square base with four depressions to hold the balls. The balls are just the right size for a small hand—the hand stretches across the ball and a fingertip grasp is needed to remove the ball. Putting the ball in is easy. Later the toy can be used as an early color matcher.

Kiddicraft/2/*Price Code A*

Treasure Cube

This soft-sculpture cube is made of brightly colored foam-backed fabric. Inside are three soft noisemakers— a squeaky star, a rattling ball, and a chiming cylinder. The items are put in and taken out through slits in two of the cube's faces. A variety of objects can be put inside; it is best to start with small rigid plastic or wood items so that the child can really feel the object inside the soft walls of the box.

Baby Dakin/2/*Price Code B*

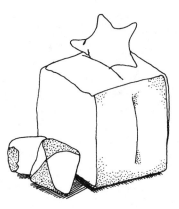

POUNDING TOYS

Pounding starts early. A child starts pounding as an infant, banging cup against highchair tray or rattle on coffee table. This is the first step toward becoming a tool-user. A great mental leap has been made: the baby has understood the implication of banging two things together. It is a leap we should marvel at and use as a starting point for constructive pounding activity.

Baby's Rhythm Band

At much the same time children are interested in exploring busy boxes, they are also developing their ability to bang, pound and use a beater to bang with. This unusual busy box combines exploring and banging. Each of the four activities on this stable box are activated by banging with the small beater. Bells ring, a xylophone chimes, colored balls jump under a see-through drum, and "gumballs" dance under a see-through dome.
Battat/2/*Price Code B*

Knocky Block

Knocky Block consists of a rectangular plastic box with four holes in the lid, a concealed ramp inside, and a trough along the outside. Pound a ball through the lid, the ball comes out of the box and rolls down the trough, ready for another turn. The Knocky Block comes with four sturdy plastic balls, so it is easy to set it up with only one ball to work on at a time. A secondary game with this toy, which a child discovered for us, is possible when the lid comes unglued. The toy can then also be used as a tracker. Put the ball into the now open box and *watch* it roll down the interior ramp, through the hole, and down the trough.
Ambi/2/*Price Code B*

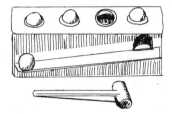

Flip Around Pounder

Pounding on one end of this pounding toy causes wooden disks to flip up and over a hoop. A large turning wheel can be pounded on or turned by hand, producing a good loud ratchet sound. The hammer enclosed is a perfect length for a small child.
Playskool/1/*Price Code B*

Slapsticks

A pounding bench with a difference: the pegs to be pounded are plastic and decorated as little men. Once all the men are pounded down, the bench is turned over and the child starts again.
Ambi/2/*Price Code B*

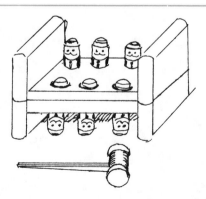

PEGBOARDS

As a child's ability increases, pegboards are used for fine motor control, visual perception, and hand-eye coordination. Putting a peg in a hole is a very basic wrist rotation task, too. Because they are valuable for building so many skills, pegboards are used again and again. Many different pegboards are included here so that they don't become boring. Having the child's active interest is the beginning point for all learning.

Pop-Up Toy

If you could buy only one pegboard, this would be it. The pegs are painted as little men, in primary colors. A safely concealed spring causes the men to pop up and out of the pegboard when pressed. A great motivator for putting the pegs back in! Can also be used as an early color matcher.
Galt/2/*Price Code B*

Simple Jumbo Pegboard

This simple wooden pegboard has a bright blue base and natural wood pegs. The pegs are large and rounded on one end—so they stand up only if put in correctly.
Lakeshore/3/*Price Code A*

Play Posts

This unique toy is a cross between a puzzle and a pegboard. Brightly painted, easily recognized shapes are fastened to the top of chunky pegs. The pegs are inserted into an oblong pegboard. This toy is wonderful for children who do not have the fine motor control needed to rotate a puzzle piece into place but who are bored with conventional pegboards.
Skill Builder Toys/3/*Price Code B*

Eye-Hand Coordination

This is the Rolls-Royce of early pegboards, in both quality and price. But because it has multiple uses, it is recommended. The 12 pegs are large and slightly knobbed on the grasping end. Painted in very bright true primary colors, they can be put into the box-like base at random, or colored sliding panels can be put on the base to be used for color matching.
ETA/3/*Price Code D*

Color Pegboard

A pegboard that is used for color matching and big/little concept as well as the usual pegboard skills. Ten pegs of five bright colors: five big and five small; the pegs are put into the long base in color pairs.
Whitney Bros./2/*Price Code B*

Big-Little Peg Kit
We don't often think of giving children black toys, yet when you see this you'll understand how effective black can be. The base is a black box with six interchangeable black lids and nine colorful pegs: three large, six small. All lids and pegs can be stored in the box. Lids progress in difficulty and the colors show brightly in contrast to the base.
American Printing House for the Blind/3/*Price Code C*

Color Pegboard
This is a 25-hole pegboard that is child-sized. Only 7 inches square, the base is a heavy hardwood, the pegs are in five colors and of graduated lengths, so that the task can progress from simply putting the pegs back in, to putting them in rows of matching colors, to putting them in color *and* size order. The pegs are painted with glossy enamel and children find them very appealing.
Brio/2/*Price Code B*

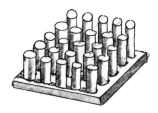

Tactilemat Pegboard and Easy-Grip Pegs
This is the pegboard most frequently used with young children (sometimes it's the *only* pegboard used, and that's boring). The pegboard has 25 holes and is made of crepe rubber. The easy-grip pegs fit right into a small palm. Because the base grips the pegs tightly, we use this for helping with muscle building among children with low muscle tone. They have to really *pull* to get the pegs out. Quite a bit of skill is required to put the pegs in, so the set has a long life-span.
Ideal/2/*Pegboard*   *Price Code A*
　　　　　Pegs   *Price Code A*

Big Pegboard

The pegs and holes in this 25-hole set are quite small, so skills must be well developed to use it. The base is black, so the colored pegs show up in contrast. The special feature with this board is that each peg has a hole in the top that another peg can be put into. Some children have stacked all 25 pegs atop each other, making a tall, bendy tower.

Discovery Toys/3/*Price Code B*

Sort, Build and Count

This pegboard has 25 square pegs in beautiful color-stained wood. The challenge of working with square pegs while sorting by size and color is enough to keep the older child interested in the task.

Childcraft/3/*Price Code C*

SHAPE BOXES

Shape boxes are the next step after pegboards. Once a child has developed the coordination to place a peg in a hole, the task then becomes learning to discriminate shapes enough to place a shaped peg or form into a hole of the same shape.

When choosing a shape sorter, keep the child's ability and interest level in mind. It's probably best to avoid shape sorters that have more than five or eight basic shapes. By the time a child is able to discriminate between an octagon, a hexagon and a pentagon, the child will probably have lost interest in shape sorters.

Shape Sequence Box

Many sorting boxes present such a confusing array of shapes that the child gives up before mastery can be achieved. Not this one, a simple wooden box with five interchangeable sliding lids progressing in difficulty from one shape alone to five shapes together.
Constructive Playthings/3/*Price Code B*

Lock-a-Block

Except for the locking door, which is almost always impossible for a very young child, this sorting box is terrific. The three shapes (circle, square, triangle) are three-dimensional—sphere, pyramid, and cube—so that whatever face of the shape the child presents, it will drop into the box. The locking door has its positive side, too—it assures parent/child interaction. Brilliant primary colors in indestructible plastic.
Ambi/2/*Price Code B*

Simple Sorter

A simple drum-shaped sorter with an easily removed three-hole lid. Shapes are three-dimensional—sphere, pyramid, and cube—and a good chunky size.
Lakeshore/3/*Price Code A*

Shapes & Slides Playground

Three animal-headed shapes fit into the top of this sturdy play center. Once in their correct place, a push on a broad button causes the animals to slide down and out of the box. The animals can also be given rides on a shape-coordinated merry-go-round.
Fisher-Price/1/*Price Code B*

Shape Sorting Box

A box within a box; the open-topped solid-faced wooden box acts as a holder for the inset box, five faces of which have holes: one, two, three, four, and five respectively. The holes and blocks are in geometric shapes; the blocks are bright primary colors.
DLM/3/*Price Code B*

Jumbo Shape Fitter

This almost could be classified under pegs. But this is a pegboard with two differences. First, each of the four pegs is a different shape: circle, triangle, square, and rectangle. Because the shapes are long, like pegs, the child doesn't try to put the shape in sideways, as is so often the case with shape sorters. Second, the shape pegs can be pushed through a tunnel in the base, which adds to the fun.
Lakeshore/3/*Price Code A*

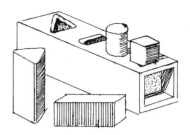

Sound Puzzle Box

The top of this see-through cylindrical box has openings of three different shapes. The shapes to be sorted are unique: not only do they each have a handle to hold on to, but the handle is painted as a little face, and a safely concealed squeaker causes the shape/man to squeal as it sldes down into the sorter. Language-enriching play is possible, and children are so fascinated with the squeak that they'll sort the shapes over and over.
Battat/2/*Price Code B*

Sorting House

This shape sorter is excellent because of the many possibilities for language enrichment. The wooden box is painted as a house. Various shapes are put in through the windows, doors, and chimney. Because of the sloping base of the box, the shapes slide right down to the bottom, ready to be put in again.
ETA/3/*Price Code C*

Shape Sorter Transporter

This big sturdy plastic truck provides the base for many shape-sorting activities. The three shapes fit into the inside of the hatch doors on the back of the truck. All the shapes can be stacked onto one another. Two cylindrical "people" add to the possibilities for imaginative play with this creative toy.
Johnson & Johnson/1/*Price Code B*

Shape Shop Surprise

A visual reward is given for correctly inserting one of the four shapes onto the playboard. A fan whirls, a television picture changes, a telephone rings and the hands on a clock advance. The shapes are particularly easy to handle.
Tomy/1/*Price Code B*

Kaleidosort

This is a magnificent sorting box for the slightly older child. There are five shapes on top and a sliding Plexiglas panel in front. The inside walls of the box are covered in mirror-like foil paper, so that each shape dropped in can be looked at through the front panel and be seen reflected by the interior walls. All these extra features can be too dazzling to a distractible child, but can be enough to capture the interest of a child who is bored with shape boxes.
Childcraft/3/*Price Code C*

Turn-n-learn Key Sorter

This shape sorter combines the skills of sorting by shape and turning a key with the visual and auditory rewards usually associated with busy boxes. Sturdy plastic keys with different shaped bases are inserted into the correct area of the box. Turning the key activates an activity. For example, colorful gears turn around each other with a ratchet sound, a rabbit wobbles back and forth, or eggs rotate around a chicken.
Battat/2/*Price Code B*

STACKING TOYS

Stacking toys are difficult. If pegboards can be defined as challenges for putting pegs into holes, stackers are for putting holes on pegs. The problem is that the hole is so small and is surrounded by a solid so that it's difficult to see where the hole is. Much coordination and skill is required to center that hole onto that peg.

Stacking toys are available in a multitude of shapes and sizes. From a three-disk stacker with a dog's head to a mammoth 20-piece stacker of graduated sizes and rainbow colors, all are geared toward accomplishing the same task: putting holes on pegs. When choosing stacking toys, think about the number of pieces; fewer is probably better. Choose stackers that don't require the disks to go on in any particular order, because they won't.

Rainbow Stacker

This wooden stacker has a rectangular base with four pegs, each with five disks on it. Each peg and its corresponding disk are a different primary color. The task thus becomes color matching as well as putting the hole on the peg. Although the disks are graduated sizes, they rarely go on in any kind of order.

Environments/3/*Price Code B*

Stack 'n Pop

This is a marvelous stacker. Once the six half-spheres are put on and the trigger set, the child can push a lever and a strong spring pops the spheres off the peg. A great motivator for putting them back on!
Discovery Toys/3/*Price Code B*

Big Bead Stacker

There are many difficult tasks involved in this stacker. Spheres are used instead of disks and they are difficult to put on. Most of what the child has learned about how to put a hole on a peg won't work with spheres. Additionally, the pegs are graduated in size so that they accept only from one to five balls. The balls are colored but the pegs are not, so the child has to count and find which color he has only one of and put it on the shortest peg. Used as it is designed to be used, this is a size/color/number stacker. Of course, it can be used simply to help with the difficult task of finding a hole in a sphere and putting it on a peg, ignoring everything else. The other skills can be taught later, when the child is ready. This set has flexible pegs for safety and comes with vinyl tubing, so there is an additional activity—the beads can be threaded.
Laplandia/2/*Price Code B*

Color/Shape Abacus

Exceptionally beautiful colors, shapes, and a good texture combine to make this stacking toy a favorite. Ten clear bright colors—including pink, black, white, and brown—come in ten shapes, and can be sorted in many ways. Because the ten stacking spindles are on two separate bases, it is possible to limit the task to fit the child's interest level by only doing five at a time. The stacking pieces are quite small so should not be used with a child who still explores with his mouth.
Childcraft/3/*Price Code C*

Pattern Stacker

This is one of the most advanced stacking toys we've found. The base has red, blue, and yellow pegs, graduated disks, and 20 pattern cards. The task is to match the disks to the pattern cards, *on* the pegs. Cards progress in difficulty.
Childcraft/3/*Price Code C*

PILING/NESTING TOYS

Super Building Beakers

These 12 cups are beautiful bright primary colors; three each of red, blue, yellow, and green. The cups can be stacked into a tall multicolored tower, or each color can be stacked into a small tower. Each cup has a lip on the bottom that helps the child with the difficult task of no-topple stacking. Part of the fun of course is knocking the tower down as soon as it's built, and then the child delights in nesting the beakers inside each other. This is a beautiful toy with rich play possibilities.

Kiddicraft/2/*Price Code A*

Hand Cones

With a coat of nontoxic paint and a layer of nontoxic varnish, these heavy cardboard cones become a sturdy, colorful fine motor toy. The cones are easy to stack, either onto or into each other. They are also fun to talk into, listen into, and look through!

ADLaides/3/*Price Code A*

Castle Tower Stack Up

The five cylindrical cups of this toy look like castle towers. When they are all piled together, a little king goes at the top. Nesting the towers afterwards is fun, too.

Combex/2/*Price Code A*

Stacking Baskets

Twelve small brightly colored plastic baskets nest into one another. A lip at the base of each basket helps with the job of stacking. It's great fun to play with these in water, watching the water come out of the holes. It's also fun to play peek-a-boo through the holes.

ETA/3/*Price Code A*

Pull Disks

Five wooden disks fit into the base of this nesting toy. Each disk has finger-holes in it to help pull it out of the base block. The smallest has one hole, the largest has five, so some counting play is possible, too.

Childcraft/3/*Price Code B*

Stack'n Fit School

Two open-ended cylinders fit inside two narrow square containers, which fit into two rectangular containers. All these shapes fit into a larger square container with a roof-shaped lid and a school decal on the front. There are many possible combinations for stacking and nesting. Children also enjoy playing with the cylinders separately—looking through them and talking through them is fun!

Johnson & Johnson/1/*Price Code B*

TWO-HANDED TOYS

Many children with handicaps have difficulty using two hands together at midline. Whether one hand is being used to help stabilize the child's body, or one hand simply does not work very well, or midline organization does not come easily, using two hands is often a therapy goal. These toys require two-handed play. For children who have no difficulty with two-handed play, these toys are just good fun.

Audible Animals
A cow, a horse, or a chicken make quite a loud animal sound by simply pushing down and releasing the head. The child's other hand is used to stabilize the animal by holding onto its back.
Tomy/1/*Price Code A*

Jack-in-the-Ball
This variation on a jack-in-the-box is a winner. The jack fits into a small weighted plastic ball. A push-button triggers the jack to pop out. Pushing him back in causes a squeak. With one hand stabilizing the ball and the other pushing the button and pushing the jack back in, this two-handed toy is fun. It can also be played with as a ball, although its weighted base makes for a wobbly roll.
Ambi/2/*Price Code A*

Nature Shells
Inside each of the six realistic-looking eggs in this set is a little rubbery animal. As the egg is opened, the animal pops out. Children love tapping the egg on the table edge (as they've seen Mom do so many times), using two hands to open the egg, and discovering the animal inside. The eggs store in a sturdy plastic egg carton.
Small World/2/*Price Code A*

Wrist-a-Flex

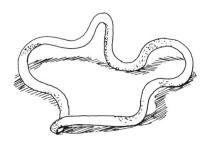

Although intended for therapeutic activities, this unusual brightly colored plastic ring is fun to play with. The jointed sections can be turned, twisted, and coiled into many weird shapes, all while providing wrist rotation exercise.
ADLaides/3/*Price Code B*

Acrobats

These brightly colored plastic people can stand individually. Their arms can be clicked around the body of another acrobat, or their legs can be clicked onto the head of one of the others, *or* they can be clicked onto one of the horses that comes with the set. Sorting by color and counting, two-handed play and imaginative play are all possible with these attractive, sturdy plastic figures.
Childcraft/3/*Price Code B*

Clic-a-Wheel

When two hands grasp and rotate the protruding handles on this small disk, a wonderful clicking sound is produced. Although it is somewhat difficult for a young child to learn how to work this toy, the challenge and reward make it fun. This is one of the best toys for two-handed activity and wrist rotation.
Kiddicraft/2/*Price Code A*

Mr. Twist

Many twisting/threading toys have limited play possibilities. Once the job of twisting is done, the toy is put aside. Mr. Twist is different. Language play, as his various body parts are talked about and then threaded, and imaginative play with the finished product are all possible. The pieces go on and twist down very easily.

Kiddicraft/2/*Price Code A*

View-Master

This traditional toy is still around with picture disks available on every subject from Sesame Street to Michael Jackson, the Muppets to Scenic Wonders of the Grand Canyon. Today's children are just as fascinated looking through the two eyepieces to see a picture and clicking the lever down to advance the picture disk as their parents were. Most children are so excited by this toy that they forget they're using two hands together at midline!

View Master/1/*Viewer Price Code A*
Picture Disks Price Code A

Cone Puppets

Cone puppets have been a standard toy in Europe for many years. The body of the puppet is pulled down into the cone by holding the stick with one hand, the cone with the other. A simple game of peek-a-boo can be played as the puppet pops out of the cone. With older children, more elaborate dramatic play will evolve. By twisting the stick the puppet moves from side to side; quick up-and-down tugs on the stick make the puppet dance. Available in an amazing assortment of characters, including animals, witches, and people of all ages.

Battat/2/*Price Code A*

Other two-handed toys in this book are:

Jumbo Stringer
Tube Stringer
Tool Slinger
Ring of Charms
One Dozen Eggs
Slinky
Wonder Blocks
Bristle Blocks
Colormonica
Rikki Tikki

THREADING TOYS

Threading beads is very skillful play. One of the first two-handed activities, it requires mastery of the pegboard idea—putting a hole on a peg—but here the peg is flexible and doesn't have a base. The problem with most bead-and-lace sets is that the lace is *too* flexible. The child's skills usually aren't finely enough developed to enable him to hold the tip of the lace right at the tip, so the lace flops and it is impossible to insert into the bead. The lacing sets included here are quite easy.

Tool Slinger

Young carpenters don't make any noise with this unusual tool kit! Eight recognizable tools are made of crepe foam rubber. The flat colorful tools are strung onto a ring of thick vinyl tubing, which is fastened by plugging one end into the other. The large holes in each tool make threading a success.
Lauri/2/*Price Code A*

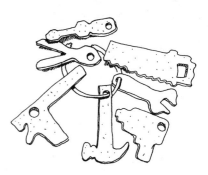

Ring of Charms

Eight large colorful crepe foam rubber shapes and eight smaller squares are threaded onto a thick piece of vinyl tubing. Because the pieces are such recognizable shapes—a duck, a key, a teddy bear— there are many possibilities for language play with this fine motor toy.
Lauri/2/*Price Code A*

Jumbo Stringer

The "lace" in this bead set is made of vinyl tubing of quite a good size. It is possible to hold the tubing quite far down and still be successful at getting it into the hole in the bead. The 12 wooden beads are large and very brightly painted.

Laplandia/2/*Price Code A*

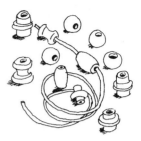

Tube Stringer

This set is similar to the one above, but both beads and tube are smaller. Twenty-five beads.

Laplandia/2/*Price Code A*

Beads and Baubles

The many "beads" in this set are unique: they're made of crepe rubber and they're almost flat. The hole is a good size, although the string is too floppy and should be replaced—NG tubing would be good. But because the beads are so flat the child has a good chance of getting the lace through before it flops. Children love the crepe rubber texture, too.

Lauri/2/*Price Code A*

CONSTRUCTION TOYS

Bristle Blocks

Because of the design of the blocks, Bristle Blocks are among the easiest construction toys. Each plastic block is covered with stubby plastic bristles. (They resemble old-fashioned hair rollers.) The bristles interlock with each other with very gentle pressure. Most sets come with wheels and some of the larger sets come with faces that can be built into people.

Playskool/1/*Price Code B*

Wonder Blocks

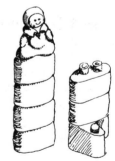

These interlocking blocks are ideally shaped for little hands. The pastel plastic has enough texture that the blocks aren't slippery. The blocks come in variously sized sets, some of them with little Eskimo people.

Mattel Preschool/1/*Price Code B*

Snap 'n Play School Pack

These multishaped wooden blocks connect to each other with snap buttons. Advanced fine motor skills and good finger strength are needed, but kids love the challenge of this unusual construction toy. A building board with 16 snaps is also available to provide a working surface for building.

Lakeshore/2/*Blocks: Price Code B*
Building board: Price Code A

Builda Helta Skelta

This is an action-packed construction toy. A large assortment of brightly colored plastic ramps can be built into any configuration desired. Then the fun begins! Marbles are dropped into the top, and their descent, accompanied by loud clattering, is watched. This is a difficult toy to figure out, as the ramps have to be strategically placed, but even if Mom or Dad does most of the building, it's great fun for the young child to put the marbles in, watch them go down, and retrieve them at the end. Not safe for a child who still puts everything in his mouth.

Kiddicraft/2/*Price Code B*

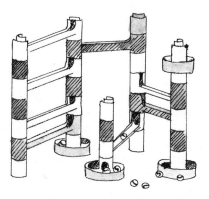

DESIGN AND PATTERN SETS

These toys require a high degree of fine motor control. They also require that the child be able to abstract: see a picture and copy it. Older children with good manipulative skills love using them to make patterns. It is best to start these toys with the child building directly onto the pattern card. Only much later will the child be able to make a pattern alongside the card.

Some of the following block and pattern sets have pattern cards that increase in difficulty, with the early ones being quite simple, the later ones very complex. The child can either make patterns directly onto the pattern card or build them up on the table, using the pattern card as a guide. The sets are uniformly beautiful, with wooden pieces dyed in clear, bright colors.

Magneton

This toy makes playing with shapes, colors, and patterns accessible for the younger child or the child with limited fine motor control. Brightly colored solid plastic magnetic shapes are played with on a good-sized magnetized white board. Design ideas are included. The shapes can be pushed around the board or taken off to be placed. **Marlon**/2/*Price Code B*

Colored Inch Cubes

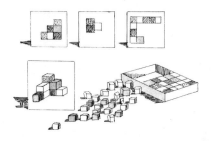

These 96 one-inch wooden cubes are glowing colors: red, blue, yellow, green, orange, and purple. They can be used by themselves for sorting and stacking or with the pattern cards below. **DLM**/3/*Price Code B*

Colored Inch Cube Designs

Thirty-two laminated cards progress in difficulty. Very appealing.
DLM/3/*Price Code A*

Beginner's Frame Mosaic

Beautifully colored, smooth
wooden pieces fit into a see-
through plastic grid. Children enjoy
simply fitting the pieces into the
grid and creating their own designs
or using the pattern cards (sold
separately) to copy designs.
Because the grid is transparent,
the design card can be put
underneath, making the pattern a
bit easier to follow.
T.C. Timber/2/
Frame Mosaic Price Code B
Pattern Cards Price Code A

Large Parquetry Blocks, Large Parquetry Designs

The 32 blocks are three basic shapes: square, diamond, and triangle,
and the same six colors as the inch cubes above. There are 22 cards in
the design set.
DLM/3/
Blocks: Price Code B
Designs: Price Code A

OTHER FINE MOTOR/VISUAL PERCEPTION TOYS

Jack in the Box

This is one of the best jack-in-the-boxes available. The knob for opening the lid on the sturdy wooden box is exceptionally easy to operate. The box lid pops open with a quiet bell-jangle. The "Jack" is a wooden-headed clown puppet attached by a Velcro patch to the lid. The clown has bright blue nylon hair just right for little fingers to dig into to pull off the Velcro and get the clown out of the box. A bell is firmly attached to the clown's neck. It's wonderful to see a tiny child go through the whole sequence: operate the knob, pull the clown off, shake it so the bell rings, be helped to put the clown back on, and close the lid with two hands, anxious to start again. Highly recommended.

Laplandia/2/*Price Code B*

Pop-up Pals

Squeezing the box on this soft sided jack-in-the-box causes it to pop open. The little character inside can be taken completely out of the box and be squeaked by bouncing it against a firm surface.

Playskool/1/*Price Code A*

Tracker 1 and Tracker 2

Push the wooden ball through the rubber gasket-lined hole on top of this large wooden box and then watch it roll down the ramps inside and come out a hole at the bottom. The dark background helps make the ball visible the whole way down. Expensive, but often this is the only toy that will fully engage an on-the-move distractible 2 year old. Great for helping with tracking skills and concentration span. Available in 2 sizes.

Salco/3/

Tracker 1: Price Code G
Tracker 2: Price Code F

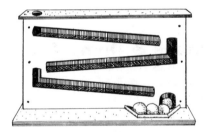

Rings and Rollers

Two see-through cylinders and two rings fit together in many combinations. The great fun with this toy is watching the beads roll down the spiral ramp inside the cylinders.

Johnson & Johnson/1/*Price Code B*

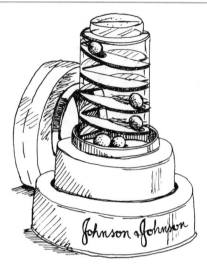

Stack & Dump Truck

This truck has many unique design features. Ten disks—five square and five round, in two colors—can be stacked on spindles, posted through holes in the top of the truck, put into the grid on the top of the truck on their edges, or hung from the lights or wheels. The hinged top of the truck opens easily and is designed so that fingers cannot get caught as the dumping is done. In addition to all these good fine motor skills, of course, this toy *is* a truck and great imaginative play takes place as the truck is loaded, unloaded, and driven away.

Johnson & Johnson/1/*Price Code C*

Developmental Bead Sequences

This set of four bead frames increases in difficulty, offering a variety of increasingly challenging perceptual motor activities. They are brightly colored and durable. Each frame comes with an explanatory booklet suggesting uses and vocabulary that can be used with each frame. Many varied activities and purposes are possible: color naming and counting as well as motor skills and visual tracking.

Lakeshore/3/*Price Code G*

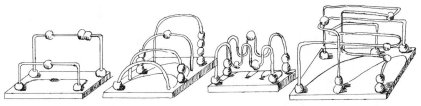

Oscar the Grouch

When you squeeze the rubber bulb, Oscar peers out of his garbage can with a squeaking noise. Although the can is mounted on wheels and can be pulled by the bulb, most children play with this as a stationary toy. Oscar is great for helping to understand cause and effect. Small children will need to use two hands to get the bulb depressed enough to cause Oscar to pop out.

Fisher-Price/1/*Price Code A*

Lots-O-Gears

Although there are several gear sets on the market, this is our favorite. The base is covered with black nylon, and each gear-wheel has a spot of Velcro on the back, so the gears can easily be placed in many configurations. Most of the 12 gear-wheels have a hole for inserting the drive peg, so again, the child can decide where to put it. By starting the child off with just one gear and the drive peg and intermeshing the gears from there, the toy becomes a science experiment with the dual purpose of wrist rotation.

Childcraft/3/*Price Code B*

Snapazoo

This flat velour shape with eyes has snaps around its edge. Many animal shapes—both real and fantastic—can be made by snapping the snaps together in different combinations. There is no "right" way to do the snaps, although instructions are included for making 25 different creatures.

Procreations, Inc./2/*Price Code B*

GROSS MOTOR

GROSS MOTOR PLAY

Gross motor play is dependent on head, trunk, and limb control in many positions—sitting, standing, climbing, running, jumping, throwing. A normal child achieves this free and fluid movement through movement itself. Beginning with lifting his head off the floor, then head and chest, then rolling and crawling, pulling up, sitting and standing, cruising and walking, running and climbing, jumping and kicking, throwing and catching, each accomplishment is achieved with hours of practice and many near-disastrous bumps and falls, each skill leading from and to other skills. Toys help the child refine these skills and achieve mastery. The most important provisions for gross motor play for a normal child are the space to move in and someone to kiss away the inevitable bumps.

A child with a handicap is not as likely to develop in this straight-line progression. Children with any serious deficit in motor, mental, or sensorial development may experience a delay in movement, or may progress toward movement only through intensive therapy. Yet it is through movement that a child begins to experience and understand the parameters of his world—its size, shape, color, hardness, softness, height, depth—all of these are explored through stomach, knees, feet, hands, and head when moving. The impaired child will need an adult's help to experience movement, to pick him up and take him to new experiences, and to help him find comfortable positions for play. As time goes on, the child may need adult encouragement to move and explore. Toys can help with this, serving as the prop the adult uses to get a child moving with confidence.

It should be stressed that all of these toys should be used with adult supervision, both to enhance play and ensure safety.

EARLY MOVEMENT TOYS

Peek in Roller

This toy isn't very durable, but it is worth rebuying. An 18-inch inflatable cylinder, the roller has transparent panels to enable the child to look inside and see the brightly colored balls. It makes a great exercise bolster for a tiny baby and can also be used for peek-a-boo and shaking by an older child.

Childcraft/3/*Price Code A*

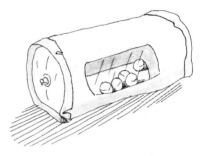

Giant Tumble Balls

These durable inflatables come in three sizes: 21, 26, and 38 inches. They can be used as therapy balls to help learn muscle control, motor coordination, and balance. Lighter than the noninflating therapy ball, they can be bounced by the larger child.

Lakeshore/3/*Price Code B-D*

Bean Bag Chair

For small children, a bean bag chair is a wonderful gross motor toy. Crawling over it is a real challenge. For the older child the chair makes a great target for jumping into, or even a cozy place to curl up with a book.

Lakeshore/3/*Price Code D*

Little Carriage Horse

This wooden rocking horse has a chair back and arms built onto it, making it completely stable for a child who needs lots of support. The barely curved rockers add extra stability, making it possible to do quite gentle rocking; ideal for a child who is tentative about controlling her body.

Schowanek/2/*Price Code F*

Toddle Tune Rocker

For the very young child, this rocking toy has many appealing features. The seat is built up at the back so the child won't slide off while rocking, and a gentle chime is activated by the rocking. The low center of gravity makes this rocking toy feel safe for even a timid child.

Lil Tykes/1/*Price Code B*

Fun-L-Tunn-L

Crawling is good exercise and good fun. This collapsible 9-foot cloth tunnel is pale blue denim, and quite indestructible. Children are often reluctant to go in by themselves at first, but this tunnel is big enough for an adult. A child will almost always crawl in when Mom is the goal. The pale blue allows a great deal of light to come through, and it makes the inside a very calming place to be.

Constructive/3/*Price Code C*

Educubes

These sturdy plastic chairs are bright primary colors and can be used as chairs, desks, or giant building blocks. The design is superb. Placed on one face of the cube, the chair is a good height for a baby or young child; placed on another face, the chair is low enough for an older child. The chairs have good deep backs and arms which lend trunk support. Outstanding!

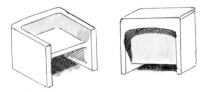

Learning Products/3/*Price Code H*/*set of 4, sometimes available singly.*

WALKING TOYS

Baby Walker

This little wooden cart has a handle affixed at a right angle—it is almost impossible to tip over. A child can crawl over to it and pull himself up on the handle without causing a disaster. Extra stability can be added by putting some bricks into the cart. Children who are on the verge of walking will take off and walk with this cart in front of them. Because of its boxy shape, however, the cart doesn't steer well. The child will walk until he hits a wall or piece of furniture. She will learn to steer quite quickly, but be prepared for screams of frustration until she does. A word of caution: the baby walker can be used only by a child who understands and is ready for forward movement. If the child is only "cruising"—moving sideways while holding on—she'll pull up to the cart, give a push, and the cart will move on, but she won't— she'll land on her face.
Galt/2/*Price Code D*

First Wagon

This baby walker has the same overall design as the one on page 82 but is larger. The additional inches in the handle height and increased weight make it useful for the older, bigger child just learning to walk. Because of its larger size, this walker can have a long life-span as a doll carriage, and is strong enough to hold quite a big child, too.

Childcraft/3/*Price Code D*

PUSH TOYS

Often a child is able to walk, but only when holding a hand or other object. Push toys are great for this stage, lending that little bit of extra stability. Also, a child who would fall over because he can't manage the rotation required to look back to see a pull toy can manage a push toy, which puts all the action in front of him. The following are favorites. It is a fairly easy matter to modify either of them to hold a longer handle for the older child.

Corn Popper
This classic toy has a see-through dome on wheels. When it is pushed, brightly colored balls pop up and hit the dome.
Fisher-Price/1/*Price Code A*

Mower Push Toy
A large cylinder that looks like an old-fashioned push lawnmower. Several really noisy bells and balls move freely inside the cylinder when it is pushed.
Laplandia/2/*Price Code B*

Melody Push Chimes

A mellow chime rings as this classic toy is pushed. Big balloon wheels make Melody Push Chimes a particularly stable push toy.
Fisher-Price/1/*Price Code A*

RIDING TOYS

Riding toys bridge the gap between the baby walker and the tricycle. These toys are for sitting astride and pushing with your feet. Points to remember when choosing riding toys are: (1) seats are often too wide for tiny bodies, spreading the legs so far apart that the child doesn't have freedom of movement with his legs, and they can't touch the ground; (2) seats are such slick plastic that the child gives one push and slides off the back of the seat; (3) handles are too floppy for stability.

We've found these to be almost ideal.

Tiny Trike

Most riding toys have four fixed wheels and the child has to learn to steer by slightly lifting the toy and making midcourse adjustments. This trike has a T-handle attached to the two front wheels and can be steered easily. Its seat height and width are ideal for a small child. Large plastic balloon wheels lend extra stability.
Galt/2/*Price Code D*

Ride-On School Bus

A bright yellow school bus is a meaningful symbol to even a young toddler. He'll enjoy putting the removable driver in the front of this little yellow bus, lifting the seat to stow a favorite toy and hopping on to drive off on *his* bus.
Fisher-Price/1/*Price Code D*

Hot Rod Roadster

This riding toy has a tractor-type seat so the child's legs are quite free. The handle is a steering wheel that spins, but doesn't steer—*and* it has a horn. The Creative Coaster can also double as a wagon, as the base is a rectangular box that comes with some plastic building blocks, and the steering wheel handle can be brought forward and pulled. A word of caution: Because the handle can be brought forward, it isn't as stable as it should be in the driving mode. You might want to adapt it for complete stability, although this would eliminate its second use as a wagon.

Fisher-Price/1/*Price Code B*

Adapted Tricycle

A child can be put on a tricycle quite early. At first, the adult will do all the work, just giving the child rides and letting him feel the movement. Later the child will learn how to push the pedals, giving him mobility and some independence. With the tricycle adaptations available from *The Equipment Shop, PO Box 33, Bedford, MA 01730,* a child with physical impairment can be given the trunk, foot, and even leg support needed to give him access to the world of bikes.

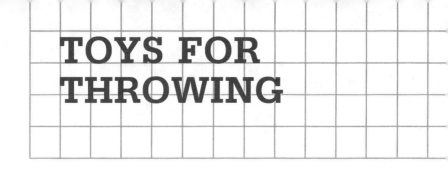

TOYS FOR THROWING

Dr. J. Basketball Set

This free-standing basketball hoop is on a telescoping pole which adjusts the height so that a nonambulatory child can play while sitting or a walking child can play standing up. The soft foam ball makes indoor play safe.

Ohio Art/1/*Price Code B*

No Miss Mitt

Throwing is easier than catching, and it's a long time before some children have the control to catch. This game will help with that. A Velcro baseball glove is paired with a smallish ball covered with Velcro loops. The child needs only to move her arm to bring the glove into the general target area and the ball will stick on.

Childcraft/3/*Price Code A*

Art Darts

A target game. The Velcro-covered board has an ice cream cone with the numbers from one to five in different areas on it. The child throws the Velcro-covered ball at the target and it easily adheres.

Lakeshore/3/*Price Code B*

Wacky Bat and Ball

This all-foam bat and foam ball can be used safely indoors or out. The wide surface of the bat helps ensure that contact with the ball *will* be made. The squishy foam handle maximizes the strength of a weak grip.
Childcraft/3/*Price Code A*

Nerf Basketball

An indoor basketball game that can be played almost anywhere! The "basket" frame hooks on to the top edge of a door, but will also slide onto a chair back or hook over the edge of a kitchen drawer. The foam ball bounces nicely and is soft and safe.
Parker Brothers/1/*Price Code A*

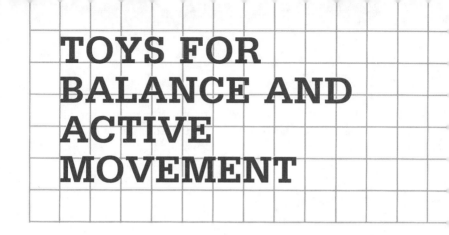

TOYS FOR BALANCE AND ACTIVE MOVEMENT

Balancing is a challenge. From the early days when the baby lying on his stomach shifts his weight from one arm to the other and still manages to keep his head upright and his eyes focused, to the time when a child rides off on a two-wheeled bicycle, there are many stages in refining the ability to balance with movement. These toys provide the child with the opportunity to experiment with balance in new ways. As with all gross motor toys, adult supervision is essential. With Balance and Active Movement toys, the adult is needed not only for safety, but to help the child develop the confidence needed to master these fun but sometimes scarey toys.

No Fail Streamers

Waving ribbons like these is a new Olympic sport. Nine feet of brightly colored taffeta ribbon is attached to a stick handle with a nontangling swivel. Wonderful patterns are made with the ribbon by waving the stick around. As the stick is waved the child does a lot of weight shifting and balancing without being aware of it. This can even be used while sitting (although it does get tangled more easily), making it possible for nonwalkers and babies to join in the fun.
Lakeshore/3/*set of five Price Code C*
each Price Code A

Turbo Spinner

This is a ride-on toy that doesn't go anywhere. A bright yellow car body with realistic decals sits on a low, geared base. Turbo spinner will turn in the direction the steering wheel is turned. Children get the impression of traveling, and of speed. A built-up back lends some support.

Kaye's Kids/3/*Price Code C*

Sit and Spin

It is very difficult to describe how Sit and Spin works. Many children learn how to do it by watching other children. Basically a one person merry-go-round, the child sits on the ground-hugging base, which spins as he tugs hand over hand on the fixed central column. Because it is so close to the ground, most children are not afraid to get on and give it a try.

Kenner/1/*Price Code B*

Hippity Hop

This is an inflatable ball with an attached head with handles. The child sits on the ball, holds on to the handles and uses his legs to bounce and spring around. Great fun!

Sim Products/1/*Price Code B*

Graduated Balancing Board Set

There are three balance boards in this set, ranging in height from 1 to 3 inches. Young children feel very proud of being able to balance on even the shortest board. Taller boards can be used as confidence grows.

Lakeshore/3/*Price Code D*

Foot Stomper Set

Some children are so unsure of their gross motor abilities that they choose to always play while seated. Foot stompers may help coax them out of their chairs. Basically a little catapult, by stepping on one end of the Stomper, a bean bag pops off the other end. The set has two Stompers—one is used with one foot, the other with two. As the child gets more confident and more skilled, he can attempt catching the bean bag as it pops up.
Lakeshore/3/*Price Code A*

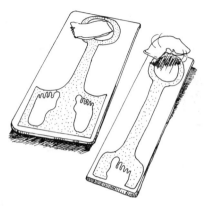

Roller Skates

These brightly colored, nonbreakable plastic skates are easy to put on with Velcro straps, and have a lock mechanism so that they will only roll forward when the child is first learning to use them. Children love them. One little boy went to sleep with them next to his bed and insisted on skating to breakfast!
Fisher-Price/1/*Price Code B*

Romper Stompers

This plastic version of tin can "stilts" is fun for the older child. The child stands on sturdy plastic inverted cups and holds onto the attached ropes. With careful coordination (and lots of practice!), the child will be able to walk forward.
Playskool/1/*Price Code A*

AUDITORY/
MUSICAL

AUDITORY/ MUSICAL TOYS

Almost all children respond positively to sound. Even children with a severe hearing loss love sound if it's loud enough or of the right frequency or has enough vibration to feel. In talking about sound-producing toys, we think about three kinds of toys: (1) passive toys that the child listens to with or without visual reward; (2) active toys, which the child acts upon to create the sound; and, (3) passive toys that the child listens to with a goal, such as matching the sound to a picture. As one might expect, it is the active toys that are the most thrilling. Because the child is so engaged with them, active sound toys can be used by the teacher/therapist/parent for other purposes: fine motor control, hand/eye coordination, large arm movements, and working at midline, to name a few. It is important to remember, however, that these other purposes are *your* goals. The child is interested only in sound production, and it should be fun.

PASSIVE SOUND TOYS

Sesame Street Musical Box TV

This music box is shaped like a television, and pictures move across the screen as the music plays. It's a perfect height for putting on the floor while a prone baby lifts his head to watch the pictures. A handle on top makes it very portable for the toddler.
Fisher-Price/1/*Price Code B*

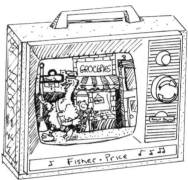

Tote-A-Tune Music Box Radio

This small portable radio-shaped music box has a handle for carrying, a "station changer" sliding button on the side, and small pictures that appear as the music plays.
Fisher-Price/1/*Price Code A*

Music Box Clock-Radio

Children love the springy antenna on this portable clock-radio music box. The clock face rotates as the music plays, and it has a carrying handle.
Fisher-Price/1/*Price Code A*

Phonograph

This is an extremely sturdy monaural record player with reasonably good sound quality.

Fisher-Price/1/*Price Code E*

Tape Recorder

A battery-operated tape recorder, this is almost indestructible. Good sound reproduction and easily pushed buttons make this ideal for the young child. It comes with a tape which has a sound-effect story on one side and is blank on the other for recording your own sounds.

Fisher-Price/1/*Price Code E*

Books and Tapes

Most children love listening to stories, and there is a growing number of book/cassette tapes on the market. Fisher-Price makes a large assortment of hardbound books with accompanying tapes. A storage envelope for the tape is mounted on the back of the book. The titles range from *Three Little Pigs* to *Superheroes.* Golden Books has an increasingly large selection of titles. Their books are paperback and will need storage in a zipper-locking plastic bag. We have also had tapes made for some of our simpler story books.

Records

Listening to music is as important to a child as it is to a teenager or an adult. There is a huge variety of children's records on the market. Don't be limited by the children's section, however. Children enjoy marching bands, jazz, and classical music, too. Some favorite children's vocalists are Raffi, Hap Palmer, and Ella Jenkins.

ACTIVE SOUND/ MUSICAL TOYS

Cluster Bells and Wrist Bells

We use these rhythm band instruments as musical rattles for very small babies. The bells are very firmly mounted on chewable plastic, and are loud with good tone. Babies who are still mouthing all their toys really love the coldness of the steel bells.

Rhythm Band/2/*Price Code A*

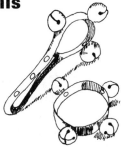

Tambourine

A real tambourine with skin surface, steel ringing disks, and a wooden frame is one of the best early music toys, because it can be used in many ways. Very small babies will get quite a resonant response by scratching the skin surface. Tapping on the surface gives a drum-like sound, and causes the ringing disks to make some noise. As the baby gets older and stronger, satisfaction will be had by banging the wooden rim against the floor—the disks really jangle then. And, of course, the tambourine can be used as it was intended, as a rhythm band instrument, by the slightly older child.

Environments/3/*Price Code A*

Little Player Piano

A simple push on any one of the three broad "keys" on this small plastic music box causes its tune to advance by one note. The piano can be banged with the whole fist, thus making it accessible for the very young child who can't yet turn a knob or push a small button. Great for cause and effect, too.
Tomy/1/*Price Code A*

Big Mouth Singers

A child needs very little strength or control to get a big response from this battery-operated toy. Basically a piano keyboard, pressing a key causes one of the Muppet-like faces on top to open its mouth and make a bell sound. Made of plastic, it is surprisingly sturdy. Kids love it, mothers don't because it is quite noisy, and not a particularly pretty noise. But it *is* fun!
Child Guidance/1/*Price Code B*

Melody Parade Piano

Banging on the keys of this piano/xylophone hybrid causes plastic hammers to strike the xylophone bars. Although banging produces the loudest sound, it is possible to get quite a good sound by gently pressing the keys. Children will discover that another way to play is by flicking the hammers directly. Surprisingly sturdy.
Davis—Grabowski/2/*Price Code B*

Tap-A-Tune Piano

This colorful piano/xylophone has several very distinctive features. The rainbow-colored keys are far enough apart that a young child intent on making music won't be frustrated by hitting more than one note at a time. There is a built-in carrying handle. Although no beater is included, the xylophone on top can be played with a beater, adding to the enjoyment of this toy.
Little Tykes/1/*Price Code B*

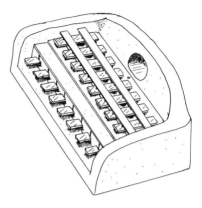

Xylobell Tree

A child becomes a tool-user when he is able to bang things with an object other than his hand. It takes a great mental leap to understand that louder sound can be made by using a tool rather than your own body. The xylobell tree is the best instrument for the onset of this stage, because the bells don't have clappers: they make sound only when hit with a beater. Eight brightly enameled metal bells hang from a tree-like central stand. They have wonderfully pure musical tone when hit with a beater, and the bright colors add visual interest. Two cautions: (1) the handles on the beaters provided are too skinny to be used by a very young child, so you'll have to provide a substitute; (2) the tree is on a detachable base and isn't very stable, so an adult will have to hold the base while the child bangs.
Marlon Creations/2/*Price Code B*

Round Bells

The clapperless bells on this musical toy are mounted on a circular frame that spins when it is pushed. The bells are metal, enameled in beautiful bright colors, with good clear tone. Good-sized beaters are included, and sound can be made in two ways: either by striking the bells or by holding the beater rigid and spinning the whole frame. Early problems of durability have now been corrected.
Battat/2/*Price Code B*

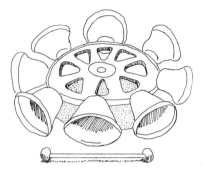

Xylo Pipes

This is a favorite xylophone because of its purity of sound and the size of its striking area. With most xylophones, the child must strike the metal between the two fastening points and sometimes that is only 2-1/2 to 3 inches long. With the xylopipes, the child can hit anywhere on the pipe and get big, pure sound. The pipes lie across a plastic base, and it usually takes no time at all for the child to discover that the pipes are easily removed. But that just enhances the toy, because then you get some nice fine-motor activity.
Marlon Creations/2/*Price Code B*

Xylo Bells

This large, sturdy musical instrument has 15 finely tuned colored pipes fixed to a sturdy wooden frame. The clarity of tone is exceptional over a two-octave range.
Childcraft/3/*Price Code B*

Little Tooter Trumpet

Essentially this is a music box. One note at a time is activated by pushing down on the trumpet keys. We usually use this with very young children, and just place the trumpet in their laps. It encourages the use of the pointer finger, although it works just as well with a whole fist or hand, too. Older children, who know that a trumpet makes sound by being blown into, are confused by the fact that blowing isn't part of the game with this toy.
Tomy/1/*Price Code A*

Little Star Guitar

The designer of this toy must have known how much little children love to use their pointer fingers to turn on light switches. This is a tiny guitar-shaped music box. A small light-switch lever causes one note of "Twinkle, Twinkle, Little Star" to be played each time it is switched up or down. A great reinforcer for pointer-finger dexterity.
Tomy/1/*Price Code A*

Marching Band

This is a good rhythm set for a young child. All of the instruments—maracas, cymbals, tambourine, and harmonica—pack easily inside the drum. Sound quality of the drum and the tambourine are only fair because they're made of plastic, but children love it anyway. The cymbals are an ideal size for a really young child to use, two hands together, at midline play.
Fisher-Price/1/*Price Code B*

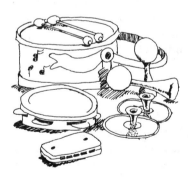

Tommy Toot

This little plastic man is a whistle. Sound is made by blowing into the hole in his hat.
Ambi/2/*Price Code A*

Rikki Tikki

This is an unusual two-handed instrument. Eighteen hardwood bars are attached to a flexible leather strip. Children roll it back and forth to produce a very pleasant clackety-clack sound. There is great tactile satisfaction in this toy.

Childcraft/1/*Price Code B*

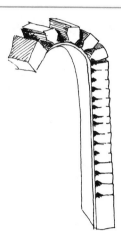

Music Box Record Player

This record player music box is quite a complicated toy. It is great for the 3 to 5 year old who understands (or needs to understand) that there is a sequence to many tasks. Put on the record, lift the arm onto the record, turn on the switch, and listen. The winding knob is recessed and is consequently very difficult to turn, so an adult will have to help. The interchangeable double-sided records store in the music box.

Fisher-Price/1/*Price Code B*

Crazy Combo

For the older child, this make-your-own musical instrument set is fascinating. Packed in a sturdy plastic carrying case, Crazy Combo is basically an instrument to blow into. By building the instrument with an assortment of different pieces, different sounds are produced. Clear step-by-step instructions are included.

Fisher-Price/1/*Price Code B*

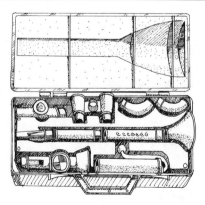

Colormonica

This is a musical instrument with a mouthpiece and a small piano keyboard. To play Colormonica, the child needs to be able to coordinate two hands at midline *and* blow into the mouthpiece *and* push the keys, all at the same time. It's challenging and fun.
Childcraft/2 or 3/*Price Code A*

AM/FM Radio

A sturdy "real" radio has been developed for children, with the added attraction of being able to broadcast through the attached microphone. The radio can be played separately, the microphone can be used separately, or both radio and microphone can be used together. Children are fascinated with hearing their voices amplified!
Fisher-Price/1/*Price Code D*

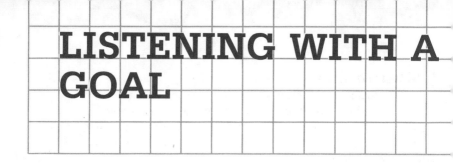

LISTENING WITH A GOAL

See and Say

Mattel makes a multitude of these "talking" toys. Set the dial to the desired picture, pull the string, and a corresponding series of sounds is made. A favorite is the animal sounds See and Say. The pictures are reasonably clear and the sounds quite realistic. The string is hard to pull, so the younger or less capable child will need help.
Mattel/1/*Price Code B*

Look/Hear

Beautiful color photos are matched to the sounds on the cassette tapes of this looking and listening game. The sounds are played twice on each side of the tape. The first time each sound is accompanied with a narrative: "The baby is crying." The second time all the sounds are played through without narration. Because the pictures on separate cards can be spread out, a child with a motor handicap can eye point to the correct card as he hears the sound.
Childcraft/3/*Price Code C*

Listening Lotto

This is a beautiful listening game. A Lotto board with clear, individual pictures on a grid corresponds to a cassette tape. When the sound of a baby is heard on the tape, the child covers the picture of a baby on the board. Twelve sounds on each of four boards correspond with 48 sounds on the tape. It may be necessary to stop the tape while the child hunts for the picture, or even rewind and replay so she can hear it again.

Lakeshore/3/*Price Code B*

Listening Lotto—Set 2

In this Listening Lotto, the items making a sound are grouped in a scene, so it is a little more difficult than Set 1. For example, the scene of a house has the sounds of a toilet flushing, a child running downstairs, a telephone ringing. The child has to find the correct room. The picture scenes are done in color and are quite clear, although the street scene may be too difficult. On the back of each scene is a grid with individual pictures that correspond to the sounds. Although these pictures are in black and white, some children find it a helpful first step to see the pictures in isolation and *then* look for them in the scene.

Lakeshore/3/*Price Code B*

TACTILE

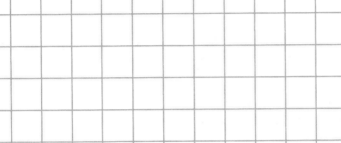

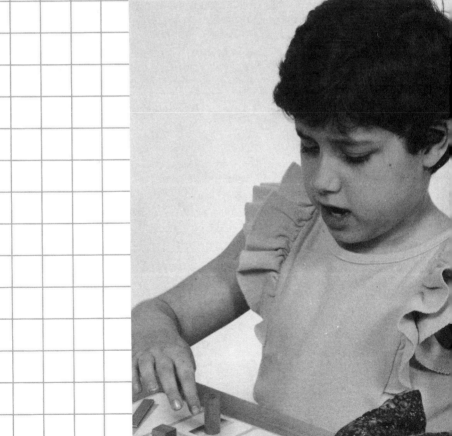

TACTILE TOYS

Tactile stimulation, leading to tactile sensitivity, is important for all children. A normal child provides her own tactile stimulation through movement. As a small infant she scratches and paws different cloth textures—the softness of blankets, the silky blanket binding, the plastic of the changing table mat, Mother's skin and hair. When rolling starts, the baby gets to feel the texture of carpet, wood floor, maybe even grass. When a child begins to creep, she is hand-to-floor much of the time and feels the differences in temperature between carpeting and the linoleum floor in the kitchen, the warmth of a sunny window— life becomes very texturally interesting.

For the child with special needs, many of these experiences don't just happen. Life is pretty well confined to the safety and softness of a blanket on the floor, blankets in bed, Mother's lap and arms, the car seat, and the changing table. Movement to explore even these areas may not be possible. It is up to the parent to either bring interesting textures to the child or bring the child to interesting textures. Let them feel these textures with face and hands and body. Make a few strips with differently textured fabrics, papers, plastics, and woods. Use a hot-water bottle or plastic jar to let her feel hot and cold. Sandpaper, fake and real fur, hair brush, cosmetic brush, metal, feathers can be used—the list is endless. They are all available to the adult, and not to the impaired child. Tactile stimulation kits are available through special education supply catalogues, but creative thought will allow the parent to make up her own kit, at far less expense, thus giving the child a rich variety of tactile experiences.

TACTILE AWARENESS TOYS

The following are all games that call for quite a high degree of tactile discrimination.

Tell by Touch

Each 1-inch wooden disk is topped with a different texture (sandpaper, corduroy, satin, etc.) that matches the texture inside the hole in this 5 × 12-inch wooden board. Although children will probably match visually, as each texture looks quite different, you can focus their attention on the different texture, thus building up an awareness of texture and of some of the vocabulary that goes with it. Later you could try the same board with the child blindfolded.
Constructive/3/*Price Code A*

Bag of Feelies

These ten pairs of 2-inch textured pieces (sandpaper, fake fur, wool, etc.) come in a sturdy cloth bag. One of each pair is put in the bag; the other is left out for the child to feel and then find the mate inside the bag by just feeling. It is best to start out with only two or three pairs at a time so it isn't too confusing.
Lakeshore/3/*Price Code A*

Bag of Shapes

Ten pairs of wooden geometric shapes are used in the same way as the feelie textures above, but it calls for more refined discriminatory skill.
Lakeshore/3/*Price Code A*

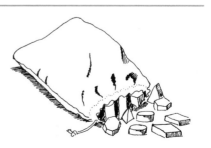

Tactilo

Twenty-five small wooden forms are contained in a bag; the child reaches into the bag, identifies the form by touch, and places it on the correct spot on one of five game boards. The forms are smoothly finished and of unusual shapes. This is our most beautiful tactile discrimination toy, and also the most difficult because of the oddness of the shapes, and because the child is matching to a picture of the shape, rather than being able to feel the matching form. It is best to use only one game board and its corresponding shapes at a time.
ETA/3/*Price Code B*

LANGUAGE
PLAY

LANGUAGE PLAY

Play must be enjoyable, and language play is no exception. Bathe the child in language. Not a waterfall of endless chatter, but a steady gentle stream of meaningful words that will help the child become better able to interpret and interact with his world.

The best language toys are the old classics—balls, blocks, dolls and doll houses, and everyday household objects. These are the language tools for normal children, and with an adult acting as playmate and guide, these can be language tools for impaired children.

To be meaningful, language stimulation must be playful. It's no good doing picture flashcards over and over expecting it to make a difference. That method may prove too much for the child to absorb; it has too little meaning. Put those words in a play situation: "Look at this *big* doll. Hasn't she got a dirty face? Let's wash it with this warm water. Look how clean it's getting." It's more fun and meaningful for the child *and* for the adult than a pile of flashcards. Parent/therapist/teacher is playmate *and* teacher.

When looking for language-stimulating toys, first consider the possibilities of general toys. "General Toys" (the Fisher-Price sink, stove, and dolls' house, airport and airplane, for example) can be used very effectively to help a child improve his language skills.

The following is a selection of games/cards/materials that meet our criterion for a language toy: they can be used playfully. Also included are some flashcards, because they are so beautiful. But these cards should be used with the child the same way a book would be read: a no-stress, no-testing, warm situation of adult and child looking at pictures together. The adult, because she knows more, is in charge, sharing information with the child, *not* testing the child's knowledge.

LANGUAGE GAMES

Bruna Memory

This memory game can be used very early as a vocabulary game. The pictures are by the artist Dick Bruna and are clear and unambiguous. The common, everyday objects and figures on the cards are in bright primary colors and stand out well against an uncluttered white background. They can also be used as a visual perception toy—can the child see the difference between the red strawberry, red tulip, and red apple?

Ravensburger/2/*Price Code A*

Bruna Lottino

This game serves as vocabulary cards and a classification game as well as an early lotto game. Each lotto board has a different type of picture—one is things to wear, one is food, another is animals, etc. The illustration is done by Dick Bruna and is crisp and clear.

Ravensburger/2/*Price Code A*

Simple Wooden Lotto Set

There are many lotto games on the market, some better than others, but all with the goal of matching the pictures on the playing board until all pictures are covered. This lotto game is particularly beautiful because the pictures are simple and colorful and both pictures and board are wood. Can also be played as solitaire.

Lakeshore/3/*Price Code B*

Picture Lotto

Very detailed color illustrations of common objects make this lotto game particularly beautiful. Because the pictures contain so much detail they may be too "busy" for a young child, but older children will enjoy this set.

Galt/2/*Price Code B*

Find It Lotto

On each of the four playing boards is a different scene. For example, one shows the inside of a kitchen, another the outside of a toy and candy store. Small sturdy cards showing the individual objects are matched to the corresponding object on the big card. Children have to do very careful looking to find some of the objects, and usually make a little sound of delight when they are successful.

Galt/2/*Price Code B*

House & Garden

This is a beautiful language game for almost any age child. Square cardboard tiles are assembled in the tray provided to make any kind of garden-scene mosaic the child wishes. The picture on each tile is printed from edge to edge so that it "meshes" with whatever is laid next to it. The scene can be mostly garden with flowers, grass, pond, fish, trees, etc., or it can be mostly house with children playing outside, etc. The variations are endless.

Ravensburger/2/*Price Code B*

Race to the Roof

Although this can be played as a competitive game, it can easily be used as a prop for wonderful language play. Race to the Roof has a large playing board of a four-story apartment house. Onto this board go picture tiles of the rooms inside the building: each floor has a living room, kitchen, and two bedrooms. Smaller cards contain single objects from within the rooms, and finding these objects is a real challenge. A beautiful game.

Ravensburger/2/Price Code B

Front/Back Memory

The first way to play with this set of cards is to simply find the matching front and back of each picture, with a limited number of cards face up. Later, it can be played as a memory game with the cards face down, and the players picking up cards randomly, trying to find matching pairs.

Milton Bradley/2/Price Code A

What's Wrong Cards/Sets 1 and 2

It's wonderful to hear a child's language ability grow; these cards are great for that. Each picture has something obviously wrong on it: a man in the bathtub with suit and hat on, a telephone with a banana for a receiver, etc. At first the child will laugh and point to the wrong thing. Later he'll say "banana." Later still he'll say the whole thing: "The phone has a banana where you talk." Kids love these cards, which appeal to their zany sense of humor. They also seem to draw comfort and confidence from recognizing something done wrong deliberately.

Lakeshore/3/Price Code A

Odd Man Out; Association Picture Cards/
Set III
These games are easier for today's children to understand because of
the Sesame Street song, "One of these things is not like the others."
There are pictures on each long strip, and one of the four or five
objects doesn't belong—carrots on a card with only fruits, Jello on a
card with only toys. The concepts are quite advanced, so should be
used only with slightly older children.
Odd Man Out: Lakeshore/3/*Price Code A*
Association Picture Cards: DLM/3/*Price Code A*

Classification Concept Photos/*Sets 1 and 2*
These are very beautiful sets because each card is a full-color photo.
The sets can be used in many ways, one of which would be to create
your own "one of these things is not like the others" game. Each set
has 30 color photos divided into six separate groups.
Lakeshore/3/*Price Code A*

The Classification Game
Four stand-up store interiors with
clear illustrations give clues to
classifying the 48 picture cards. For
example, the kite goes in the toy
store, the bread in the food store.
Once the cards are sorted, a
shopping game can be incorporated
into the play.
Instructo/2/*Price Code B*

Inlay Lotto
An excellent prereading game, Inlay Lotto has six playing boards, each
showing half of six pictures. The corresponding inlay cards show the
other half of each picture. The pictures fit into a recess on the playing
board, so they won't slide around the board as the game is played.
Jumbo/2/*Price Code A*

SEQUENCING GAMES

Sequencing: Before and After

These two-step cards have clear pictures that serve as a beginning for helping children understand time and change. They are a beginning to sequencing: "First we have a birthday cake and then we cut it."
Lakeshore/3/*Price Code A*

Let's Learn Sequence

This is a wonderful sequencing set because it has a good assortment of three-step sequences progressing through six-step sequences.
Instructo/2/*Price Code B*

Sequential Picture Cards/*Sets I, II, IV*

These sequence sets progress from a sequence of three in Set II to a sequence of six in Set I. The pictures are clear and the cards 5-1/2 × 6 inches—an unusual but nicely manageable size.
DLM/3/*Price Code A*
      Each Set

GENERAL VOCABULARY CARDS

All-Purpose Photo Library/*Set 1, Set 2*

These are beautiful sets of picture cards. Each set has over 250 large (6-3/4 × 8-3/4 inch) photos divided into categories such as animals, body parts, food, seasons and weather, and toys. The cards are stored in a sturdy storage case. The only reservation about these cards is that they aim at quite a high experiential level—the sports equipment, for example, is at least middle-school equipment. Maybe a Set 3 will be created that aims at a baby's or young child's world. Nevertheless, these are beautiful sets.

DLM/3/*Price Code F*

Naming Names

These 30 cards are pictures of common objects for young children and are nicely illustrated.

Ideal/2/*Price Code A*

Naming Actions

Most vocabulary cards are pictures of nouns. These 30 cards are clear pictures of verbs.

Ideal/2/*Price Code A*

NUMBER
MATERIALS

NUMBER MATERIALS

Children are exposed to numbers from a very early age. Most parents count with their child: they count as they go upstairs; they count as they put Cheerios on the high-chair tray; they count the number of blocks as they're stacked into a tower. Educational TV programs such as *Sesame Street* focus on counting and numerals, as well as language development. Many children's songs involve counting: "This Old Man," "One, Two, Buckle My Shoe."

Most children have at least an awareness of number before they start school at age 5. Number then becomes a curriculum subject, and some number work is done every day, starting with counting and counting objects, numeral recognition and numeral-quantity association, writing numbers, and finally number functions: addition, subtraction, multiplication, and division.

When choosing number materials we must consider that the preschool child is receiving number-awareness stimulation in his everyday environment. It probably isn't necessary for a 3 or 4 year old to be involved in number work beyond being aware of number and knowing that number words have a function. There are many other more important areas, most notably fine-motor control and language.

Once the child is in school receiving competent daily instruction in number, its properties and functions, the free time a child has is short and very precious. When a child is home from school at 3:30 and in bed by 8 or 8:30, should these few hours be spent on repeating school curriculum? Probably not. This is a time for low-key peer play and warm, low-pressure parent play.

Many playful number activities can be devised by parents: a treasure hunt where they look for twos—two shoes, two combs, two hats; making trains with blocks and counting the cars; and using number words like smaller and larger. Numbers are all around us and are part of a child's world. These number materials are additional stimulation, not a substitute for creative use of what is already present in the child's environment.

Concept Train

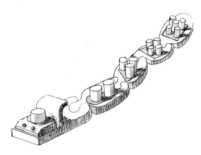

This interlocking wooden train has five cars, each painted with a number from 1 to 5, and a different color on top. Pegs of corresponding colors and graduated diameters fit into the holes in each car. And for those children who always manage to lose at least *one* peg, a set of replacement pegs is available for only $2.00!
Environments/3/*Price Code B*

Teddy Bear Counters

One hundred little molded plastic bears in four bright colors are ideal for many homemade games of sorting and counting. Children find these bears so appealing that they will often invent their own games of sorting and counting.
Milton Bradley/3/*Price Code B*

Peg Number Boards

Ten sturdy crepe rubber boards are numbered from 1 to 10, and each has the corresponding number of holes. Large-handled easy-grip pegs are included, and the child puts six pegs into the six board, three pegs into the three board, etc. The earliest number-quantity association manipulative.
Ideal/2/*Price Code C*

Number Hands

These are counting puzzles dealing with numeral-quantity association. Each finger on the hand has a numeral on it and under each finger are the corresponding number of dots. One hand has from one to five, the other six to ten, allowing the adult to limit the goal to a manageable one. The bright rainbow colors add visual appeal.

Puzzle People/2 or 3/*Price Code B/set*

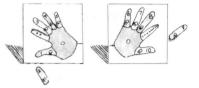

Orange Grove Abacus

This beautiful wooden counting set comes packed in a sturdy wooden box. Ten boards each have a picture of a tree on them, with ten holes in the tree. Small orange and yellow pegs are included. A dot and a numeral in the corner of each board tells how many oranges go in that tree. Because each board has the same number of holes, the child must be at the stage where she understands that one dot means one orange or that the number 4 means just four oranges. Kids love the challenge.

Doron Layeled/2 or 3/*Price Code B*

Counting Bug

This knobbed inset puzzle is a picture of a caterpillar. Each body piece is numbered, from one to ten. The inset board has corresponding sets of dots to help guide placement.

Puzzle People/2 or 3/*Price Code B*

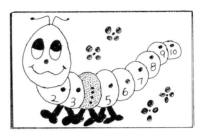

Peg It Numerals

Ten cut-out wooden numerals are each painted a different bright color and each is drilled with its corresponding number of holes. The child must match both the color of the peg and the correct number of pegs into each numeral.

Lakeshore/3/*Price Code B*

One Dozen Eggs

This is a wonderful manipulative. One dozen realistic plastic eggs are packed in a plastic egg box. Each egg separates, revealing pegs and holes numbered from one to twelve. The goal is to match the halves, and it is self-correcting. This is a two-handed toy, and because the eggs look so real, wonderful, imaginative language play can develop.

Child Guidance/1/*Price Code A*

Fonda: Number Association

This unusual teaching aid is constructed entirely of wood. The tray is grooved to hold the stand-up clue board, which is numbered from 1 to 5. The child places wooden picture cards in the grid under each number: two birds under the 2, four flowers under the 4, etc. Children love handling the wooden pieces, and the idea of working on a grid is somewhat new and intriguing to them.

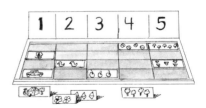

Childcraft/3/*Price Code B*

Foam Dice

These 6-inch cubes are made of foam rubber with bright red dots. Rolling these dice is easy. They can be tossed, or knocked over, or even just squeezed and released, allowing them to fall and roll. The 3/4-inch dots are an excellent size for use by a young child who still needs to count the dots.

Lakeshore/3/*Price Code A*

Picture/Number Lotto

Knowing how to count by rote is very different from understanding that three means three of something: numeral-quantity association. In this simple lotto game the child matches a picture quantity to its corresponding numeral. Nicely illustrated.

Galt/2/*Price Code B*

Jumbolino

By rolling the dice and matching the number of dots to the playing pieces, an interlocking clown is created. An early counting game, Jumbolino has the added features of being very beautiful *and* dealing with body parts, color, and left/right.

Battat/2/*Price Code A*

Know Your Numbers

The wooden puzzle pieces and colorful illustrations make this numeral/quantity association game very appealing. A number jigsaw puzzle is assembled as the lotto board is completed by matching pictures to numerals:
Play Plus/2 or 3/*Price Code B*

Plus and Minus School Bus Game

The goal of this little game is to move a school bus "counter" from school to home by using a spinner marked with plus numbers and minus numbers. The playing board is fun to assemble because it is made of pictures of store fronts on sturdy cardboard. Part of the fun of this game is simply setting up the town before starting the homeward journey.
Edu-game/3/*Price Code A*

Pirates' Gold

A race game on a sturdy playing board. Simple addition and subtraction problem cards help or hinder in reaching the treasure.
Galt/2/*Price Code B*

Sneaky Snake

The challenge is to build the longest snake possible, using the dice to match snake parts. One-to-one relationships and lots of counting make this a good early number game.
Growing Child/3/*Price Code A*

Numbers Up

Pegs numbered from 1 to 20 are fitted into the holes in a plastic boxlike frame. The game is played using a built-in timer which causes the pegs to fall in under the box if all the pegs aren't inserted before time runs out. The ticking of the timer may seem too frantic when just learning how to play—it's a good idea to let the child have a few turns playing without the timer.
Milton Bradley/1/*Price Code B*

Puzzle Math

Colorful puzzle pictures are created by correctly playing this unusual math game. Each of the four puzzles is constructed by matching the number on one side of the cards with the number shown on the dice. Completing the game gives the reward of turning the cards over to see the picture.

Leisure Learning/2 or 3/*Price Code A*

PLAYING GAMES

PLAYING GAMES

There are two main types of games: games of make-believe, which include both solitary and cooperative pretend play, and games with rules, which include most of the commercially available board games.*

Board games become appropriate when the child is about 4 years old. It is at this age that a child understands and can tolerate waiting his turn, playing according to external rules, fair play, and sharing (also losing, although most young children find this particularly difficult). Early board games need simple rules and a quick finish, not allowing a child to get bored.

Although most of these games can be put into other categories such as *language* or *number concept,* they have been put into games deliberately, because they should be used primarily for fun. Games provide a great format for getting the whole family involved in playing together and sharing fun.

*This section describes particularly enjoyable games with rules; make believe play is discussed in the General Toys section.

GAMES

Candyland

This classic game is one of the earliest board games. The goal is to take your man along the candy path. No reading is required and there are some good color-matching and square-counting skills along the way.
Milton Bradley/1/*Price Code A*

Color Balloons

This color-matching game is basically a lotto game played with dice. Roll the color dice and match that color with a balloon on your card. Although four cards with clear Bruna illustrations are included, it is best for the very young child to play with only two people at first, because waiting his turn isn't easy.
Ravensburger/2/*Price Code A*

Teddy Bear Bingo

Children enjoy the tiny three-dimensional bears used for playing pieces in this lovely little color game. A spinner is used to determine which color bear gets matched to the corresponding colored circle on the playing board.
Milton Bradley/2/*Price Code A*

Learn to Play

When a child is first learning to play organized board games, one of the most important features of a good game is that it be over quickly, because the child's attention span is short. Each game in this set of four board games can be played in just a few minutes. A good introduction to taking turns, moving playing pieces, fair play, and winning and losing.
Ravensburger/2/*Price Code B*

Insey Winsey Spider

This quick little game uses plastic spiders as the playing pieces. A roll of the dice *and* a spin on the weather dial determines how many spaces can be moved up the drainpipe to the spider's web.
Orchard Toys/2/*Price Code A*

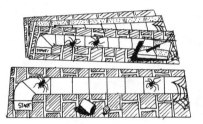

Hi-Ho! Cherry O

An early counting game. The first player to get ten cherries in her bucket is the winner. A simple spinner and small plastic cherries add to the fun. Children love this game!
Western Publishing/1/*Price Code A*

Humpty Dumpty

A beginning color matching and counting game, the goal is to match the King's horses to the King's men by color and be the first to assemble Humpty Dumpty.
Orchard Toys/2/*Price Code A*

Count-a-Color

This beautiful color matching game has short, colored wooden pegs that are placed into the playing board based on the throw of the color dice. Each player has a separate playing board which is illustrated with a different scene.
Ravensburger/2/*Price Code B*

Blockhead

This is an unusual game. Irregularly cut blocks are piled into a tower until it falls. Players take turns. Good fine-motor skills are required to pile up the tower. Great fun when it crashes.
Pressman/1/*Price Code A*

Flying Hats

Children of all ages are intrigued by this game. A small hat is placed on a little plastic catapult. An easy push on the catapult causes the hat to pop up, turn upside down and flip into the grid inside the game box. For young children, that will be the whole game. For older children, keeping score by adding the numbers in the grid will add interest.
Spears/2/*Price Code B*

Mr. Pop

This face/body parts game consists of a plastic head into which features are placed while a timer ticks. If not completed before the time runs out, it pops, and all the features pop out. A game to be played alone, it might be too nerve-wracking to have the timer going when the child first begins learning to play.

Lakeshore/2/*Price Code B*

Memory Game

There are many varieties of this game, which is played the same way as Concentration. Cards are placed face down and pairs are found through random turning over of the cards, the players taking turns. Children enjoy this game because their memories usually work as well as or better than an adult's does, so they play as equals. The simple pictures and plastic storage tray of Memory Game are particularly good.

Milton Bradley/1/*Price Code A*

Don't Spill the Beans

Each player is given a pan of little plastic beans. One by one—taking turns—the beans are put into a balanced pan. If the pan tips and the beans spill, the player who put in the last bean has to take all the spilled beans. Although the goal is to get rid of all your beans, many children love having the beans spill, and collecting the *most* beans rather than the least. It's easy enough, then, to play the game with opposite rules.

Schaper/1/*Price Code A*

Let's Eat Out

This board game uses tickets for fast foods like hamburgers, ice cream and hot dogs to move along a path to the end of the game. The game progresses quickly, and because the foods are such favorites, children get very involved in enjoying this game!

Selchow & Richter/1/*Price Code A*

PUZZLES

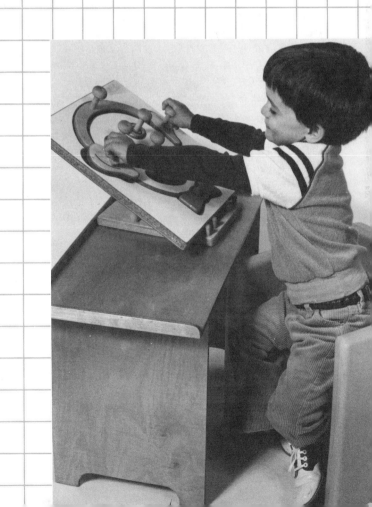

PUZZLES

A child needs access to many puzzles. Puzzles help consolidate cognitive, fine-motor, language, and perceptual skills, and children like doing them. These skills aren't easily or quickly learned, so a wide variety of puzzles keeps the child interested and learning.

Once a child has the fine-motor skills to put an irregular piece into its hole, puzzles can be used to help teach many concepts. There are excellent puzzles with pieces identical except for size. Others deal with directionality—the same chicken is on each piece, but it looks different ways. Others are for color matching. There are some excellent number puzzles, still others that deal with the alphabet. Body parts are particularly well taught with puzzles when each puzzle piece is a separate body part. There are a few excellent face puzzles on which each piece—eye, nose, and mouth—is a part.

Both receptive and spoken vocabulary can be worked on with puzzles. There are puzzles that have animals and their babies, puzzles that deal with animals and their homes. Think of almost any subject you'd like to teach a child and there will be a puzzle to go with it. And because the child is actively involved in disassembling and reassembling the puzzle pieces, you have his active attention and interest in learning. But first the child *must* be able to manipulate the pieces into the holes. Otherwise all that active attention will be channeled into the physical job of assembling the puzzle, and the concepts will be lost.

PUZZLE PROGRESSION

STAGE 1

When a child is very tiny, puzzles can be used in much the same way as pegboards: for taking things out. At this point, the puzzle isn't really being used as a puzzle. The child is learning the concept of "out" and developing the motor skills to perform this task. Puzzles for this stage are knobbed, ranging from those having pieces with huge handles which can be grasped with the whole hand, to those with tiny knobs, which require a pincer grasp, as illustrated. An ideal progression of puzzles would be:

Three Shapes

The huge handles on this puzzle fit right into the palm of a small hand. With only three shapes—circle, square, and triangle—the job of taking out will be quickly accomplished, and some nice vocabulary enrichment ("You're taking out the circle.") is possible. **Salco**/3/*Price Code B*

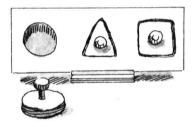

Five Pets

The animals of this puzzle—dog, cat, fish, duck, and rabbit—and the long peg-like handles combine to make this an interesting puzzle. **Judy**/2/*Price Code A*

Colored Balloon Puzzle

The knobs on this puzzle are big enough to get some palm involved but small enough for an emerging pincer grasp. The eight brightly colored circular balloons are all the same size so if the child does try to put them back in, success is usually immediate.

Puzzle People/2/*Price Code B*

Common Objects

Fifteen common objects—clock, cat, house, flower, fish, etc.—are closely arranged in three rows on this small puzzle. The knobs are tiny and require a pincer grasp. This puzzle is used as much for vocabulary enhancement as it is for fine motor development. At first, the puzzle pieces will be identified as the child takes them out. Later, the child can be asked to find a particular piece. A favorite with adults *and* children.

Simplex/2/*Price Code A*

Big and Little Teddy Bears

A large and a small teddy bear with big, palm-sized knobs fit easily into this two-piece puzzle. Children are usually quick to identify the bears, and may even try putting them back in.

Salco/3/*Price Code B*

STAGE 2

Later, when the child has the cognitive and motor skills to understand "putting in," puzzles are used in much the same way as shape sorters. Puzzles with smooth edges that don't require a lot of rotation for success and have knobs are best for this stage.

Four Fruit Puzzle

Four brightly colored fruit-shaped pieces—apple, banana, orange, and pear—fit easily into this long puzzle. The spool-like knobs help in the task of putting them into the puzzle board.

Doron Leyaled/2/*Price Code B*

Ice Cream Cone

This puzzle has only two pieces—a cone and a scoop of ice cream. With the smooth regular edges and large handles characteristic of this manufacturer's puzzles, this puzzle will be an easy early favorite.

Salco/3/*Price Code B*

Colored Geometry

Four large brightly colored geometric shapes fit easily into this puzzle. As in all of this manufacturer's puzzles, the inside of each shape's space is dark, helping with figure-ground differentiation.

Salco/3/*Price Code C*

Five Fruit

Many puzzle manufacturers make a fruit puzzle. The beautiful stained, colored wood and large knobs of this five fruit, oversize (12 × 14-1/2 inch) puzzle combine to make it a favorite.

Salco/3/*Price Code D*

Five Animals

This puzzle has five easily recognizable animals gently colored with stain. Large handles make this a favorite early "putting in" puzzle.

Salco/3/*Price Code C*

Three Ice Cream Cones

With this ice cream puzzle you can have one, two or three scoops on your cone. Three ice cream cones and six scoops of ice cream, all interchangeable, fit into the base of this big, challenging puzzle.
Salco/3/*Price Code D*

Face

This oversize puzzle is a clown face with removable eyes, mouth, hair, ears, nose, and bow tie. Children respond to the simple artwork and enjoy taking out the pieces as they are named, matching the piece to their own or the adults' face, and then putting the pieces back in. Available with or without handles.
Salco/3/*Price Code D*

STAGE 3

Once the child has good fine-motor skills, a puzzle becomes a visual perception/visual memory tool. The task is finding the puzzle shape that matches each hole. The child deserves praise for finding the hole, and then again when she manages to get the piece into the hole.

By the time a child is at the third stage in doing puzzles, handles are less important. Most of the rotation necessary to get these more complicated, irregular pieces into each hole will be done with the whole hand and fingertips at the puzzle edge. This stage would be started with, for example:

Colored Circles

This beautiful round puzzle has five circles in graduated sizes and different colors. Although no rotation is required, good visual perception skills are necessary to match the correct size and colored piece to the corresponding hole.
Salco/3/*Price Code D*

Body

This is an inlaid puzzle with seven pieces fitting into a single opening. Each piece is a body part: head, arms, legs, shirt, pants. Children love this first "big" puzzle.
Puzzle People/2/*Price Code B*

Fruit or Vegetable

Quite a bit of rotation is required to put these irregularly shaped fruits or vegetables into the puzzle board. Painted in bright, realistic colors, the fruits (apple, pear, banana, grapes, and orange) will be more familiar to a young child than will the vegetables (carrot, lettuce, tomato, corn, and celery).
Doron Leyaled/2/*Fruits Price Code B*
Vegetables Price Code B

Table Setting

This puzzle is a favorite with children and adults alike. The painted pieces are two halves of a plate, knife, fork, and spoon and are almost full scale.
Doron Leyaled/2/*Price Code B*

Snowman

Big handles and simple pieces characterize this puzzle of a snowman being built. The pieces are not true circles so require a bit of sophisticated rotation and visual perception.

Childcraft/3/*Price Code B*

Who Lives Here?

The beautifully illustrated farm scene on this puzzle has seven animal houses (pig pen, cow barn, etc). Under each tiny-knobbed puzzle piece is a picture of the animal that lives in that house. Many possibilities for language enrichment.

Victory/2/*Price Code B*

Vehicles

A picture under each vehicle of this puzzle is an added surprise. Eight vehicles, including an airplane, a car and a train, each with a tiny knob, are fun to take out and put back in.

Fisher-Price/1/*Price Code A*

Fish

Each color-stained fish on this puzzle looks a little different or faces a different way, thus requiring good perception skills to get them back into the correct space.

Salco/3/*Price Code D*

Eating an Apple

The sequence of eating an apple, beginning with a whole apple and finishing with a core is illustrated in this simple four-piece puzzle. Small knobs help with the task.
Puzzle People/2/*Price Code A*

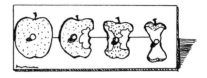

STAGE 4

More complex puzzles are used for abstract thinking: seeing a part of a whole, and knowing where that part goes. At this stage, the language involved becomes very important: not only naming the piece, but describing its relationship to the other pieces; such as over, under, next to, etc. An important point to consider when choosing puzzles for this stage is whether or not the pieces are cut along logical lines. It's difficult to talk with a child about the pieces in relation to the whole if the piece in question has part of a leg, part of the background, and part of a tail. It is much better if the puzzle is cut so that each piece is an identifiable part of the whole.

Billy Body

This large body puzzle has big chunky raised pieces with smooth, regular edges. Its ten pieces are each an identifiable body part. Because each piece is finished on both front and back, the child does not need to worry about left/right orientation: he can simply turn the piece over and fit it in.
Salco/3/*Price Code E*

Telephone

This puzzle has six pieces cut along logical lines. The receiver is a piece, as is the dial, the center of the dial, the base, and the two halves of the body of the phone. This is a fine example of this manufacturer's puzzles. Because the pieces are cut to be recognizable parts of the whole, it is easy to create the original picture.
Willis/2/*Price Code A*

Dressing Puzzles

Each piece of these small body puzzles is a body part. Left and right have to be figured out to replace the pieces. Although the pieces show the boy or girl wearing clothes, the line drawing underneath shows the child nude.
Childcraft/3/*Price Code B*

Kids

Although Kids is a formboard-type puzzle rather than an inlaid puzzle like the others for this stage, it requires such careful perceptual skills that it has been included here. It has 18 silhouettes of children in various active poses. The differences are quite subtle: one has its arms raised and feet together; another with raised arms has its feet apart. It is fun to copy the pose before putting it in the board.
Lauri/2/*Price Code B*

STAGE 5

Later, the child will be able to handle interlocking jigsaws, which require well-developed fine-motor skills and very abstract thinking capability.

Tiger

With only five pieces, this is an ideal way to start a child on interlocking puzzles. It is made of sturdy wood.
Victory/2/*Price Code A*

From Eggs to Ducks
Painting a Picture
Getting Dresses

Each of these simple interlocking puzzles tells a story. The beautiful illustrations are of a duck hatching from an egg and growing to adulthood (told in six pieces), a girl getting her smock on and painting a picture—and herself—(told in five pieces), and of a boy carefully getting dressed (nine pieces). The chunky wooden pieces are easy to assemble, and there are many possibilities for language enhancement.
Play Plus/2 or 3/*Price Code A*

Gardener/Police

There are two puzzles in this set. Each has nine interlocking pieces. The illustrations have Bruna's characteristic clarity and the sturdy cardboard pieces are just the right size for young hands.
Ravensburger/2/*Price Code A*

GENERAL TOYS/ CREATIVE PLAY

GENERAL TOYS/ CREATIVE PLAY

Children need access to a large assortment of toys that are just for play. Although we want all toys to be fun for the child to see and explore, many toys have a goal in addition—such as fine motor control, language development, or improvement of tactile discrimination. The toys categorized as General Toys have fun as their *only* goal. If while they are being played with, the child improves some skills, that's good, but it's not the main reason to use the toy.

These general toys are as important for the child's overall development as pegboards or puzzles or balance beams. Children need to be able to engage in joyful, light-hearted play, and to take delight in creating an imaginative world using these toys as props.

The child's parent can join in this play, not as instructors or teachers, but as playmates. It is sometimes hard for parents to learn to take time out from their role as therapist, parent, or teacher to create time and space for slightly goofy, free-form play. It is sometimes difficult for parents to relax and understand that time spent in imaginative play is not wasted.

Games of make-believe or pretend begin very early. By age two and a half the child has acquired enough language, both spoken and receptive, to understand quite a bit about his world. Make-believe play is the child's way of refining that knowledge and experiencing a situation again, for himself. In its early stages, make-believe play is closely linked to imitative play. The child is doing something he has seen others do and is repeating it for his own amusement. Later, far more structure and rules are added, and make-believe play becomes minidrama. Make-believe play gives a child an opportunity to experiment with the roles and rules of his culture, to play at problem-solving and handling power, sharing, and taking turns.

The tools for make-believe play are general toys. Although children will often use whatever is at hand to create an imaginary world (like the little girl who carefully rolled five marbles from the floor onto the rug because they were her horses and wanted to eat some grass), most make-believe games make use of toys that act as stand-ins for the real thing. Because make-believe play is based on the child's experience of life, many general toys are distinctly domestic.

The job of putting together an assortment of toys for make-believe play is relatively easy because toy stores are full of general toys. But caution and care are still necessary in order to have a collection of toys that will act as a springboard to creative play.

One of the major points to consider when looking for general toys is the generic quality of the toy. These toys should probably not be tied to any particular cartoon, television, or movie character. This limits the play too much. The goal in creative play is that the child imagine *himself* in the house, herself in the car. Good general toys should have a minimum of detail. The child and his playmate(s) will add layers of detail in their imagination.

Playing with toys that spark the imagination is fun. The possibilities for language enrichment are limitless. The closeness of parent and child as together they make up a story about the animals in the barn, or the fireman in the fire engine, or the people in the doll house can't be duplicated. The ability to play through some of the worries and mysteries and joys of life is made possible with good, simple, general toys.

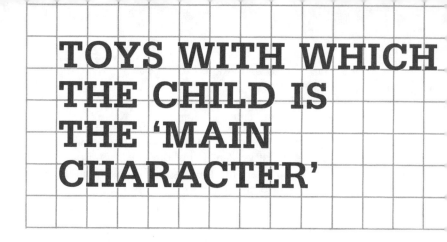

TOYS WITH WHICH THE CHILD IS THE 'MAIN CHARACTER'

In its early stages, creative play imitates life. The child is the main character in the play and the toys are models of real things in the child's environment. As the child matures, these same toys will be props for detailed dramatic play. In both cases, the child is the main character in the play.

Sink Set

Children love to play with water. This diminutive plastic sink has a chamber that can be filled with water. When the child presses on the faucet handle, the water squirts out into the sink. It is complete with drying rack, soap bottles, and enough plates and cutlery to have a tea party.
Fisher-Price/1/*Price Code B*

Kitchen Set

This little plastic two-burner stove can sit on floor, chair, or tabletop, and comes complete with pans, cups, and plates—everything necessary to cook and serve up an imaginary feast. All the parts pack into the gingham bag, which doubles as a tablecloth.
Fisher-Price/1/*Price Code B*

My Li'l Kitchen

Very young children enjoy cooking in this one piece activity-center kitchen. Toast pops up in the little toaster, an egg can be flipped using the spatula, and a pot can be stirred with the spoon. Both spatula and spoon are easily stored in a slot at the back of the play center.
Tomy/1/*Price Code A*

Bubble Mower

Jobs like mowing the lawn are fun when they are imaginary! This lawn mower looks very real and the motor sound it makes when pushed is quite realistic. The surprising feature of this toy is that when it has bubble solution in its gas tank, it blows bubbles as it is pushed!
Fisher-Price/1/*Price Code B*

Camera

Even very young children enjoy pretending to take pictures with this camera. Many will not be able to focus with one eye to see the scenes inside the viewer, but the real joy with this toy camera is in calling out "Smile!" and clicking the button.
Fisher-Price/1/*Price Code A*

Typewriter

This sturdy child-sized plastic typewriter is a favorite. The keys make a fairly realistic clicking sound, and returning the carriage causes a ratchet sound. Letters of the alphabet with a simple picture and word advance along the cylinder as the keys are pressed, adding visual interest. Mostly, however, children love just banging away on the keys pretending to be just like Mom or Dad.
Tomy/1/*Price Code B*

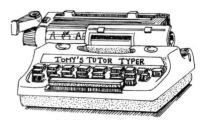

Cash Register

A good game of shopping isn't complete without a cash register. The plastic coins that come with this cash register are three sizes and colors and only fit into the corresponding slots on top. So although there are some fine motor and perceptual skills involved with this toy, mostly the child will enjoy pushing the buttons, watching the coins roll down a ramp, seeing the drawer shoot open with a bell ring, and giving it a push to close it again.

Fisher-Price/1/*Price Code B*

Medical Kit

Most children go through a stage when they love to play doctor. This medical kit, a sturdy plastic case with a handle, has usable plastic scale models of the sometimes scarey instruments doctors use. Thermometer, blood pressure cuff with Velcro fastening, "shot," stethoscope, and others all snap into their space in the case.

Fisher-Price/1/*Price Code B*

Picnic Set

Children love picnics, both imaginary and real. This child-sized picnic hamper has everything needed for a child's picnic, including a lid that can be converted into a pretend grill.

Fisher-Price/1/*Price Code B*

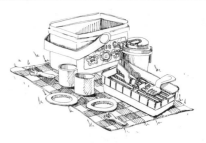

SYMBOLIC PLAY

As a child's language develops, so does his ability to engage in symbolic, imaginative play. No longer is he only the main character in the play. Rather, he can now use toys symbolically, to represent real people and objects. A tiny cylindrical character is called the Dad and he "drives" off in a tiny plastic rectangle on wheels which is, of course, a car. Children get very involved in detailed imaginative play. An interesting assortment of toys to encourage this important area of play is described here.

Discovery Cottage

There are very few toys available that meet the toddler's need to explore and his dawning ability to engage in imaginative play. This one does both. This sturdy plastic house has activities to explore on every side and on the roof. It also has two large-size Play Family figures, a puppy and an infant. The bedroom is under the roof. Both figures can ride the tricycle that is parked in the garage. There is a concealed slide down the chimney, and a favorite activity is dropping a figure down the chimney and watching it pop out the side of the house. This toy is interesting for a long time.

Fisher-Price/1/*Price Code B*

Play Family Farm

This play set has small jointed plastic farm animals with enough detail to make them recognizable. A tractor, water troughs, fences, and a few little people combine to make this farm realistic enough for even city children. The barn door opens with a resounding "Moo." **Fisher-Price**/1/*Price Code D*

Pet Shop

Young children enjoy putting the four vinyl pets (dog, cat, rabbit, and turtle) into this simple two-story pet shop. The doors open and close and the animals can peek through the windows. A built-in handle makes the Pet Shop easy to carry. **Li'l Tykes**/1/*Price Code B*

Play Family House

This first dollhouse opens from its folded position to reveal the cross-section of a house. Beds with spongy mattresses, a kitchen table and four chairs, living room chairs and a coffee table are included, as are the figures to complete a family: mother, father, two children, and a dog. There is a car in the garage. Children enjoy ringing the front door bell and rolling the garage door up and down. Often, children will unload the furniture from the house and play their game alongside in order to give themselves more space to move the tiny people and furniture around. **Fisher-Price**/1/*Price Code C*

Action Garage

Children find many play activities on this large play set. Cars can be pushed up and down the ramps, parked in the parking areas, or filled with pretend gas at the built-in gas pump. There is also a hand-cranked elevator for cars and for people.
Fisher-Price/1/*Price Code C*

Play Family School Bus

Eight little figures ride in this yellow school bus. The passengers can be put in their seats through the open roof of the bus. A side door that opens and closes adds to the fun.
Fisher-Price/1/*Price Code B*

Creative Roadway

Sturdy plastic track interlocks to form a roadway complete with a tunnel/bridge combination, a house, a garage, a car and trailer, and three little people. The ease of assembly of the track pieces and the fun of pushing the car and people around the track, up the bridge, and under the tunnel makes this toy a favorite.
Li'l Tykes/1/*Price Code C*

Play Family Zoo

Everything needed for an imaginary outing to the zoo is included in this play set. An assortment of colorful animals and trays of food to feed them, a zoo train to drive up and down the built-in ramps, a picnic table and benches for the play people to eat on all help make this large imaginary playset a favorite.
Fisher-Price/1/*Price Code C*

Creative Railway

A first train set, this railway has very easily assembled track. The train consists of three cars that are easy to hook together. The hopper car can have its load dumped. Four "people" figures come with the set and can either ride in the caboose or drive the train or dump truck.
Li'l Tykes/1/*Price Code D*

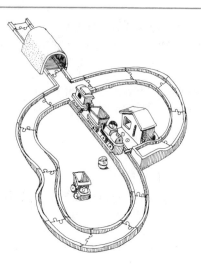

Play Transporter

This cleverly designed toy is a truck whose trailer converts into a bridge/tunnel, complete with recessed car. The truck cab can tow the car, too.
Li'l Tykes/1/*Price Code B*

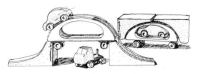

Shuffletown Farm Playset
Shuffletown School Playset

Shuffletown is an oblong play board with a play scene mounted on the board. The Farm Playset has a barn and corral which are used by two farm people and several farm animals. The School Playset has an old-fashioned schoolhouse and a merry-go-round which are used by several small children and a little lamb. Shuffletown's unique feature is that all the figures are mounted in tracks and are moved around the board in these tracks. The figures cannot tip over, fall off the board or get lost. A recessed handle makes these playsets portable, too!

Hasbro/1/*Price Code B*

Fishing Set

Two small fishing poles with magnets on the end of their lines are used to catch brightly colored wooden fish from a blue felt pond. The scale ot this fishing set is perfect for small children. All the pieces store inside a sturdy plastic box.

T.C. Timber/2/*Price Code A*

I Love My Pets Playset

The building in this playset has two sides. One side is an animal hospital, the other is a pet shop. There are lots of accessories for grooming and for playing doctor with the two little plush animals that come with the set. The doors fold up and there is a carrying handle to make this toy portable.

Tomy/1/*Price Code B*

Magnetic Theatre

This beautiful puppet theatre has tiny wooden magnetized figures that are moved around the stage with a wooden magnetized wand. Although the wooden figures are a king, queen, knight, and two small children, children quickly turn the game into a domestic scene that they identify with. The king becomes Daddy, the queen, Mommy, and the children beg to be taken out for hamburgers!
Battat/2/*Price Code B*

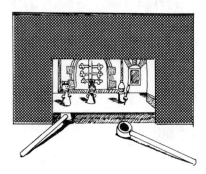

TOYS FOR CREATING

Children enjoy using all kinds of expendable art supplies: paints, markers, crayons, paper, doughs, collage materials, etc. Initially, it is the process of creating that fascinates the child: squishing fingerpaint, dribbling glue, squeezing playdough. Later on, the child becomes more interested in the product, and pays great attention to detail and to the look of the finished creation.

There are also several nonexpendable toys that give the child an opportunity to creat an end-product.

Pretty Easy Paint Set
Young children feel that they are really painting with this unusual paint set. A brush with water is all that's needed to activate the colors on the five pictures. When the water dries the colors disappear, ready to be "painted" again. The Paint Set is compact. The sturdy plastic picture cards and the brush clip into a small carrying case.
Tomy/1/*Price Code A*

Mr. Potato Head
Mr. Potato Head has undergone a few transformations in the long life-span of this classic toy and is now also available as Mrs. Potato Head or Baby Potato Head. Children create funny faces by inserting the body part play pieces into the plastic "potato" body. In addition to eyes, ears, noses, and mouths, there are now other accessories such as hats, earrings, and purses. This toy is fun.
Hasbro/1/*Price Code A*

Clay Pals

Children can create two favorite Sesame Street characters—Big Bird and Cookie Monster—with this playset. Sturdy plastic body-part pieces get inserted into nontoxic "clay" to make these stand-up characters.
Fisher-Price/1/*Price Code A*

Lights Alive

This is a battery operated draw-with-light toy. Children use the six tools included with the set to draw across the black screen, revealing the colored light which is safely concealed beneath the screen. The screen clears with a simple sliding push. Children enjoy this fascinating toy for a long time.
Tomy/1/*Price Code B*

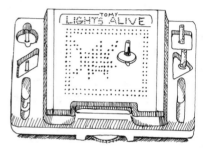

ELECTRONIC TOYS AND DEVICES

ELECTRONIC TOYS & DEVICES

In this age of video games and computers, it is appropriate to briefly discuss battery-operated toys and devices. These materials will be of two distinct types: (1) electronic toys for children with good hand and finger skills, and (2) battery operated toys controlled by switches easily operated by children with poor hand and finger skills.

Electronic Toys for Children With Good Hand/Finger Control

These materials help with listening and looking, and coordinating a response to these cues. There are many talking/teaching electronic toys on the market, and more come out regularly. Look at them. Play with them. Consider:

(a) the hand or finger pressure needed to get a response. Light pressure is best.
(b) the quality of the illustrations—does the cat look like a cat or is it wearing a frilly apron, toe shoes, and a feathered hat?
(c) the pace of the instructions/response time. Most of the children using these toys will require a slow, calm pace, at least initially.
(d) the general appearance of durability. It's hard to know for sure if a toy will stand up to hard use by children, but if it seems creaky or flimsy when new, it probably won't.
(e) what this machine does. Is it something a mother or father could do just as well, without a machine, or is this truly a technological advance?

The electronic "Simon Says" type of game, in which colored lights and sounds have to be pushed in a certain order, stimulates an enthusiastic response. Also, electronic toys that play music as a reward for pushing a button or twirling a dial are a great joy for the young child, and provide a kind of reinforcement that even a talented parent can't duplicate. Even the machines with an electronic voice giving instructions have their place in engaging a child in a task he would otherwise not do. Electronic toys, particularly of the teaching/learning variety, are still expensive, and should be purchased in person, not through a catalog. You need a chance to look, hold, play, and then thoughtfully decide if you want each toy in your collection.

Battery Operated Toys Controlled by Switches

The child with severe physical impairment has access to an extremely limited, and limiting, world of play. Unable to move his hands or arms with any accuracy, he finds toys inaccessible after he has passed the stage of infant batting/swiping toys. While ingenious parents may devise ways for the child to play by pointing to a card or playing pieces with his eyes, it is rare that a severely impaired child can really interact with toys. Rather, he is an onlooker with a passive role in the play.

The technology of electronics has changed that. Now with the aid of microswitches and subminiature jacks, even an extremely impaired child can have access to a world of playthings. Each child's ability, be it an eye blink or a head nod, can be matched with a device that utilizes that skill to turn a switch on and off. The young child can begin with a simple flashlight bulb lamp that can be turned on with the nod of a head or the gentle touch of a hand or arm, and move through a progression of battery operated toys. Eventually, the child/young teen will use his abilities, although still extremely limited, to operate a computer for environmental control, communication, and perhaps for moving his wheel chair. Learning how to operate that lamp and how to use adaptive switches to operate toys will have a direct-line connection to independent and life enriching adult skills.

An excellent book that explains this progression is *From Toys to Computers: Access for the Physically Disabled Child* by Christine Wright and Mari Nomura. This is available by writing to: Christine Wright, PO Box 700242, San Jose, CA 95170.

Dr. Steve Kanor, a biomedical engineer, has a growing assortment of adapted toys and switches available commercially. His company, Toys for Special Children, is listed in the resources at the back of the book.

Of course, no two children are alike, and each child's special need for modified devices will be very different. Linda J. Burkhart has written two excellent books that will help parents and professionals make the switches that are just right for their handicapped child. These books are: *Homemade Battery Powered Toys and Educational Devices for Severely Handicapped Children* and *More Homemade Battery Devices for Severely Handicapped Children With Suggested Activities.* These are available by writing to Linda J. Burkhart, RD 1, Box 124, Millville, PA 17846. Ms. Burkhart also explains how to adapt toys to accept the switches, making the variety of toys available to a severely impaired child almost limitless.

The *Lekotek Plan Book of Adaptive Toys* provides clear instruction on how to modify or adapt a variety of toys, including electronic toys.

With a good assortment of easily operated switches, devices, and modified toys, even a severely impaired child can be given the opportunity to engage in active interaction with a toy, giving the child the chance to be a participant, not just an observer.

BOOKS

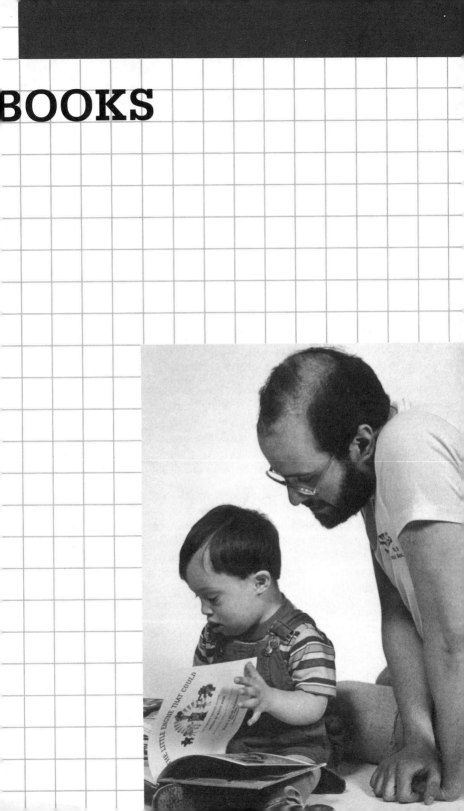

BOOKS

Books are a wonderful prop for parents and children to use to spend quiet time together. There is a warm, quiet closeness when a child sits on a parent's lap, listening to words describing the pictures. Even if the very young child isn't able to understand everything that is said, or know what every picture is, books are valuable learning materials for learning vocabulary and hearing the rhythm of speech.

When choosing books, look for books with simple, accurate illustrations and uncomplicated story lines. Many books have no story at all. These books have one picture per page and essentially serve the same purpose as picture flashcards—helping language development. The emphasis is on the illustration and the language that can flow from parent to child in talking about the pictures.

Ideally, everyone would have free access to a laminating machine and every page of every book would be laminated. But this is probably not possible, so pages *will* be torn by eager hands, and pages *will* be drooled on by an exited child. There are books available with prelaminated cardboard pages. Look at these carefully before buying them. Many use unnatural colors and their illustrations are confusing.

Among the books useful for the one-picture-per-page stage are the Helen Oxenbury board books *Dressing, Friends, Working,* and *Playing.* These have stiff pages, simple illustrations (they may be a bit too pale for children with visual impairment), and are an ideal small size for little hands. The Ladybird books from England, *Baby's First Book,* and *Picture Books 1–4* have color illustrations so detailed and clear they look like photographs. There are a limited number of early picture books that use photographs for their illustrations, and these are excellent.

Bridging the gap between picture-only books and books with words are the Ladybird *Talkabout* books. Each book has a separate topic (*Talkabout Baby, Talkabout The Beach,* etc.) and gives parents written cues about what to talk about on each page.

Fisher-Price has a series of *Discovery Books,* which show concepts such as color and opposites in a small size, laminated cardboard page format.

Books that encourage a physical involvement such as *Pat the Bunny* by Dorothy Kunhardt are rare, but worth having.

Once the child is able to manage a story line, the number, size, and quality of books available is vast. When choosing these books, look for simple books with a lot of repetition (and extremely basic plots) such as *Goodnight Moon* by Margaret Wise Brown. Stories that are within the realm of the child's experience are better than stories about tigers wearing business suits in the jungle.

Books for the young child with a disability reinforce reality rather than encourage fantasy, since one of our goals is to help the child with disabilities get in touch with and understand his world.

The best resource for books, is, of course, the library. The children's librarian has a wealth of knowledge about books and is usually eager to share this information.

Two excellent books about books for children are *Choosing Books for Children* by Betsey Hearne and *A Parent's Guide to Children's Reading* by Nancy Larrick.

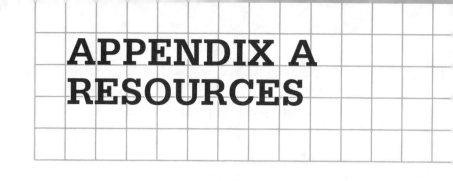

APPENDIX A
RESOURCES

RETAIL COMPANIES

These companies sell to the public at retail prices. Write for a catalog.

Able Child
154 Chambers Street
New York, NY 10007

ADLaides Co., Inc.
PO Box 2788
Glen Ellyn, IL 60138

American Printing House For the Blind
PO Box 6085
Louisville, KY 40206

Chad's Rainbow, Inc.
1778 North Plano Road
Suite 120
Richardson, TX 75081

Childcraft Education Corporation
20 Kilmer Road
Edison, NJ 08818

Childcraft: Toys that Teach
20 Kilmer Road
Edison, NJ 08818

Community Playthings
Rifton, NY 12471

Constructive Playthings
2008 W. 103rd Terrace
Leawood, KS 66206

Constructive Playthings Home Edition
1227 East 119th Street
Grandview, MO 64030

Discovery Toys
1845 Park Road
Benicia, CA 94510

DLM
PO Box 4000
One DLM Park
Allen, TX 75002

Environments, Inc.
PO Box 1348
Beaufort, SC 29902

Equipment Shop
PO Box 33
Bedford, MA 01730

ETA
159 W. Kinzie Street
Chicago, IL 60610

As a special service, Fisher-Price has a catalog and price list available to qualifying institutions spending $200 or more. This catalog can be obtained by writing to:

Dorothy Herzog
Dept. IPL
Fisher-Price Toys
636 Girard Avenue
East Aurora, NY 14052

Growing Child
PO Box 620
Lafayette, IN 47902

Kaplan School Supply Corporation
600 Jonestown Road
PO Box 15027
Winston-Salem, NC 27103

Kaye's Kids
Selected Toys & Products for Handicapped Children
1010 East Pettigrew Street
Durham, NC 27701

Lakeshore Curriculum Materials Co.
2695 E. Dominguez St.
PO Box 6261
Carson, CA 90749

Mothercare-by-Post
PO Box 145
Watford, England

Portaplay Toys
PO Box 12437
Toledo, OH 43606

ProCreations, Inc.
PO Box 27
Brookline, MA 02146

Preston Corporation
60 Page Road
Clifton, NJ 07012

Salco
Route 1
Nerstrand, MN 55053

Fred Sammons, Inc.
Box 32
Brookfield, IL 60513

Skill Builder Toys, Inc.
PO Box 873
Bettendorf, IA 52722

Toys for Special Children
101 Lefurgy Avenue
Hasting-on-Hudson, NY 10706

Toys to Grow On
PO Box 17
Long Beach, CA 90801

WHOLESALE COMPANIES

These companies sell at wholesale prices to organizations buying in quantity. Individuals having difficulty locating a particular toy can write to these companies for referral to a local retailer.

Battat, Inc.
PO Box 836
Champlain, NY 12919

Brio Scanditoy Corporation
6531 N. Sidney Place
Milwaukee, WI 53209

Classic Toys
320 Jewett Street
PO Box 223
Howell, MI 48843

Davis-Grabowski
PO Box 381594
74 N.E. 74th Street
Miami, FL

Galt Toys
James Galt & Company, Inc.
60 Church Street
Yalesville
Wallingford, CT 06492

Importoys
PO Box 34488
Los Angeles, CA 90034

International Playthings, Inc.
151 Forest Street
Montclair, NJ 07042

Laplandia Toy
PO Box 3082
Redwood City, CA 94064

Marlon Creations
35–01 36th Avenue
Long Island City, NY 11106

Reeves International
1107 Broadway
New York, NY 10010

Small World Toys
PO Box 5291
Beverly Hills, CA 90210

Schowanek
454 Third Avenue
New York, NY 10016

APPENDIX B
PUZZLE SOURCES

PUZZLE SOURCES

Manufacturer	Characteristics	Available from
Salco	Huge knobs; fine craftsmanship; few, simple pieces	Salco
Judy	Tall knobs and no knobs; good illustration; few pieces	Major educational suppliers
Puzzle People	Short fat knobs; simple illustrations; good variety of everyday subjects	Major educational suppliers
Doron Leyaled	Drawer-pull knobs; beautiful wood; fit easily	Major educational suppliers
Fisher-Price	Tiny knobs; picture under piece; some are a little too busy	Major toy stores
Willis	No knobs; cut along logical lines; simple, clear illustrations	Lakeshore
Lauri	Crepe rubber boards and pieces; huge variety	Major educational suppliers
Ravensburger	Sturdy cardboard interlocking; from 9 to 1,000 pieces	International Playthings
Playskool	Huge variety of inlaid puzzles; be careful to select logical lines	Major toy stores